The People's His

C000022887

Football in Sunderland

The Last Fifty Years

by

Peter Gibson

Hood Street Methodists line-up before the final of the All-Britain Methodist Cup at St Alban's ground, Hertfordshire, in 1960. The Street beat Abbey Wood from Kent 5-2.

Previous page: Silksworth CW Juniors AFC, 1949-50. Centre forward Stan Robson remembers: 'Silksworth Juniors were attached to Sunderland Football Club. The juniors attracted local talent and Sunderland kept a watchful eye on developing youngsters. The club saw themselves as having first choice for signing a promising young player. They used to give us strips and balls and allowed us to train at Roker Park. But scouts from other professional clubs would come to watch us play. All of the lads in the photograph were selected for trials with professional clubs.' Left to right: Stan Robson, Geordie Cutting (played for Sunderland Reserves), Tatty McIntyre, Johnny Neal (played for Hull City, Swindon, Aston Villa and Southend), Harry O'Hara, Bobby Barrowclough, Ray Snowball, Ronnie Steinberg, Sammy Thornton, Arthur Chapman (played for Sunderland Reserves) and Geordie Veitch. Mascot: Jack Walker the trainer's grandson.'

Facing page: Jonty Pemberton captain of Howard's FC, winners of the Wearmouth and Hylton Aged Miners' Cup, 1996-97.

Copyright © Peter Gibson 2002

First published in 2002 by

The People's History Ltd
Suite 1 Byron House
Seaham Grange Business Park
Seaham
Co. Durham SR7 0PY

ISBN 1 902527 94 1

Contents

Nicky Pemberton (left), manager of Wearside Combination League side Howard's FC, and vice-captain Paul Tench display the Alan Hood Memorial Trophy as winners, 1997-98 season.

This book is dedicated to all Sunderland lads who loved playing football.

Acknowledgements

I would like to thank the *Sunderland Echo* for allowing me to use some of their photographs. I would also like to thank the following people because without their help this book would not have been possible: Tom Bewick, Alan Bosher, Helen Brand, Alan Brett, Terry Briggs, R. Bucket, Bob Burke, Vera Callaghan, Tom Callaghan, Dave Callaghan, Doug Carr, John Carty, David Carty, Gordon Casey, Jack Chapman, Alan Chapman, Kevin Chisholm, Len Chisholm, Len Christopher, Andrew Clark, Harry Clark, Malcolm Clark, Tommy Clark, Joe Cliff, Dennis Colquhoun, Brian Conlon, Davie Conlon, David Craggs, Brian Cowie, Ron Cowie, Jessie Cresswell, Phil Curtis, Bob Davison, Alan Davison, Barry Davison, Colin Davison, Tommy Dobbing, Ed Downey, Barry Dunn, Peter Edwards, the late Bobby Ellens, Tony Gibbon, Bob Gibson, Mark Gibson, Peter Gibson Jnr, Billy Gilboy, Alf Goldsmith, Billy Gray, Fred Hagel, Chris Hall, Sammy Hall, Tommy Henderson, Kit Henry, Freda Hounslow, Gordon Howe, Norman Howey, George Hunter, Stuart Hunter, Ken Hutchinson, Alf Jenner, Joe Jenner, Donald Johnson, Tommy Keegan, Geoff Laws, Les Marshall, Gordon Mason, Larry McGuinness, Ray Moon, Ken Morrell, Norman Morris, Dave Mulligan, Kenny Mustard, Tony Nesbit, Tom Oliver, Keith Oxman, Peter Oxman, Nicky Pemberton, Joan Pemberton, Dave Polly, Joan Quinn, Tom Quinn, Arthur Rich, Colin Robinson, Margaret Robinson, Ray Robinson, Stan Robson, Alan Rushworth, Martin Routledge, Gordon Rushworth, Barney Sanderson, Geordie Smith, Alan Snowdon, Dave Stoddart, Bob Sumner, Harry Swindle, Tommy Thompson, Tyne & Wear Museums, Kevin Wardle, Bob Weldon, Trevor Whitehead, Billy Whittle Snr, John Wilkinson, Kevin Woodhouse, Derek Wright and Alan Wyness.

Sunderland – A Hotbed of Football

Association Football developed in Sunderland from lowly beginnings in the latter part of the 19th century when working hours were reduced enabling newly formed clubs to find the time to organise competitions and compete in leagues. The game became the most popular sporting pastime on Wearside for players and spectators alike. Sunderland teachers, some of whom had formed Sunderland Association Football Club in 1879, also played a part in establishing other association football clubs in the town. In September 1883 Monkwearmouth teachers held a meeting in the Colliery School to set up Wearmouth Association Football Club. Three months later following a meeting in Castletown Board Schools, Castletown AFC was founded in December 1883. Other clubs were created including Primrose FC from Chester Road (1884) and Curtain Wanderers from Monkwearmouth in December 1884.

Sir Hedworth Williamson was elected the first President of the newly formed Durham Football Association in May 1883 and the records show that Wearmouth, Castletown and Southwick contested with Sunderland AFC's first eleven for the Durham Challenge Cup. Clubs began to find their own level for their class of football. Sunderland joined the Football League in 1890 but there was a need for a higher standard of football in the region. The Northern League was established in 1889 and the Wearside League in 1892. Some great

Northern Alliance side Southwick Association Football Club winners of the Monkwearmouth Charity Cup in 1896-97. Three of the players and one official are wearing Durham County caps. Notice the goalkeeper back row centre wearing the same strip as outfield players. The Football Association did not introduce a different coloured jersey for custodians until 1909.

Sunderland West End Association Football Club, Monkwearmouth Charity Cup winners, 1901-02.

sides from Sunderland played in the Wearside League during the first twenty years of its existence. They included East End Black Watch, Monkwearmouth, Royal Rovers, Sunderland West End and Southwick. In 1893 Sunderland Schools' League was formed and giving local lads their first experience of competitive football before some of them achieved prominence with professional clubs.

The history of football in Sunderland is a vast subject and for this reason I have concentrated on the last fifty years though occasionally I dig further into the past. Consequently, this book is not intended to be a comprehensive history but rather a dip into the local football scene at the grass roots of our football-mad city. However, on occasion, we look into the Wearside League and Northern League, and into the professional game, and at full international level with Thorney Close lad Steve Howey.

This book covers some major achievements by Sunderland clubs: Hood Street Methodists won the All-Britain Methodist Cup in 1960, Thorney Close Youth Club were National Under-21 Champions in 1973 and Humbledon Plains Farm won the Football Association Sunday Cup in 1990.

Football is in the blood of most Wearsiders and while researching material for this book I encountered considerable enthusiasm from former players when they recalled with unabashed nostalgia their playing days in the great game at local level. Playing careers are without doubt special years. We shared the excitement of the run of the game, as well as a quality of aggression required to compete on the field of play, and of course the exhilaration of scoring a goal. Nothing compares with putting on the boots and playing football because there is no other game like it.

This book contains the images of over 2,400 players, officials and supporters of local clubs and it is hoped that readers' memories will be evoked of fifty golden years of football in Sunderland.

Peter Gibson
August 2002

SCHOOLBOY AND YOUTH LEAGUES

Hylton Red House Primary School players celebrate after winning the Durham County Primary Schools Cup, 1990-91 season.

National Fire Service Boys' Club, 1944-45. All of the boys were apprentices at Doxford's Engine Works during the war. They lived in various parts of the town and in the event of incendiary bombs landing these volunteers would cycle to the nearest fire brigade depot to alert them of the outbreak of fire.

James William Street, Division 'C' champions, 1950-51. Back row, left to right: Mr Hunter, Binyon, Martin, Hopper, Dunne, Bewick, Giles, Mr Barr. Front row: Appleby, Rich, Young (captain), Purvis and unknown.

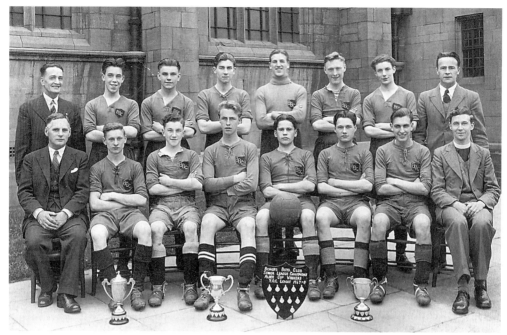

Bishop's Boys' Club, YOC Senior League champions and Alder Cup winners, 1947-48.

Sunderland Boys, 1952-53. Back row, extreme right is Peter Chape who was an England schoolboy international. Front row, second left is Alan O'Neill, an inside forward who made 76 appearances for Sunderland AFC between 1956-60 and scored 28 goals. Henry Rich (front row, centre) played centre forward for Durham County Boys and he was reserve for England Boys. He was also on Sunderland's books.

Ford & Hylton Lane Community Association, Sunderland YOC League
champions and Cup winners, 1948-49. Their home ground was Hylton Road.
Back row, left to right: Thirlbeck, Robinson, Robson, Fowler, Hedley,
unknown. Front row: O'Brien, Pratt, Marshall, unknown and Callaghan.

Sunderland AFC goalkeeper Johnny Mapson presents the YOC Championship
Cup and League Cup to Ford & Hylton League players for the 1948-49 season.

St Cuthbert's Primary School completed a splendid season in 1983 by winning their league and seven cup competitions, which included Town and County Championships. Steven Howey (captain) pictured front row, fourth from left, became a Newcastle United and Manchester City player and England international. Mick Hazard (*right*) a former pupil of St Cuthbert's and Tottenham Hotspur player presented the team with a set of strips that he bought out of £250 he received for the Robinson's South East Player of the Month award.

Hendon Sports Club Amateurs, Sunderland Amateur League winners 1946 and 1947-48.

The newly built Southmoor Technical School's three football teams line up for the 1958-59 season. Front row is the 'A' team for under-13s. Middle row is the second team for under-14s. Back row is the first team for under-15s. Southmoor School has produced some strong sides over the years and many of their boys have distinguished themselves in a higher class of football. In the front row fifth from the left is Norman Morris who was on Sunderland's books. So too was John Mellor front row seventh from left. In the middle row extreme left is Ronnie Brown who played in the First Division for Blackpool. Ron made over 60 appearances from 1965 to 1970 and scored 13 goals. His other clubs were Plymouth – 36 League appearances and 3 goals from 1970 to 1972 and Bradford City – 97 League appearances and 11 goals from 1972 to 1974. In the back row, second from left is Derek Kirby who played in goal for Sunderland Reserves. Also in the back row is Gordon Ferry, seventh from the left, a centre half who made 11 League appearances for Arsenal in 1964 before transferring to Leyton Orient in 1965 and making 42 League appearances. Jimmy Goodfellow tenth from the left played for Port Vale, Workington, Rotherham and Stockport County between 1966 and 1979. The second team in the middle progressed to the first team for the 1959-60 season and what a remarkable season it was for this talented side. Managed by teachers Arthur Coulson and Leslie Gorse they won their schools league and were Town Champions, Northumberland & Durham County Schools Cup winners, and Durham County Schools Champions. They lost only one game in 31 league and cup matches. Three members of the side – goalkeeper Derek Kirby, inside forward Ronnie Brown and centre forward Gary Moore – played for Sunderland Boys during the 1959-60 season. Gary Moore signed for Sunderland on leaving school and he made his debut against Wolverhampton Wanderers in April 1965. Gary made a total of 14 appearances for Sunderland, scoring 2 goals.

Fulwell 32nd Cub Pack, unbeaten Sunderland Northside Cub League champions and Cup winners, 1976-77. Back row, left to right: Steven Wardropper, Russell Hughes, John Morris, Karl Langley, Paul Cooke, Peter Colledge. Front row: Ian Simpson, David Wayman, Gavin Iley, Andrew Russell, Ian Smith, Gordon Hall and Steven Russell.

Bristol Aero Apprentices, 1957-58. Back row, left to right: Thompson Gill, Tommy Trusty, Thomas Grey, Tommy Taylor, Billy Gibbons, Eddie Malaugh. Front row: Les Young, Matty Ward, Dennis Steele, Joe Liddy and Harry Swindle.

Southwick Boys' Club, Alder Charity Cup winners in April 1952. Pictured with two female supporters they are back row, left to right: P. McDonough, A. Douthwaite, A. Watson, H. Thomson, C. McArdle, R. Hart, S. Bucket (secretary). Front row: J Askew, R. Currie, J. McGuinness, R. Hadden and T. Madden. In the same season Southwick BC were joint holders of the YOC Junior League Cup and were runners-up in the league to Bishop's BC.

Silksworth Colliery Welfare Juniors with committee members, 1949-50. Centre forward Stan Robson holding the ball remembers: 'I played for Silksworth Juniors for two and a half seasons and I scored over 80 goals a season because I was supplied by a very good team. There were much better players than me in the side without a doubt. We were the talk of the washhouse and when we played in cup finals at the colliery grounds and also at Roker Park the village emptied to watch us.'

Doxford's Apprentices FC, Sunderland Amateur League winners, 1951-52.

Fulwell CAYS (Christian and Youth Society), 1961-62 unbeaten Sunderland YOC Junior League champions, Michael Oxberry Memorial Cup winners, McGeorge Memorial Shield winners and the Alder Charity Cup winners. Back row, left to right: George Holt (youth leader), Goodhall, Craggs, Maddison, Hargrave, Liddle, Barker, Pillans, Bridgewood, Reg Watson (manager). Front row: J. Grieves (secretary), Murphy, Younger (34 goals), Donoghue (97 goals), Johnson and Philliskirk.

The highly talented Sunderland Boys side of 1954-55. Back row, left to right: Timm (West Park), Wright (Commercial Road), Stoddart (Redby), Jenner (St Benet's), Oliver (Bede Grammar), Rooks (Barnes). Front row: Watson (Easington), Swan (Seaham St Joseph's RC), Wynn (Ryhope Grammar), Rollason (Silksworth) and Noble (Easington). Dickie Rooks made 40 appearances for Sunderland AFC.

The strong 1954-55 Sunderland Boys side put in a serious challenge for the English Schools' Trophy. After defeating Liverpool Boys in the 7th round Sunderland Boys met Manchester Boys in the semi-final at Roker Park on a windy Easter Monday in 1955. The lads were losing 1-0 from a tenth minute Manchester goal until five minutes from the end when Jubb, the Seaham Camden Square outside left, powered in a strong header to equalise. The *Echo* reported: 'The half backs in both teams had a good day with Oliver and Jenner prominent for Sunderland … The strong wind did not prevent these boys giving a talented display but it proved too much for their team mates.' The replay at Manchester ended in a 2-2 draw after extra time and Roker Park hosted the second replay on Friday 6th May in front of an official attendance of 18,378. Sunderland went ahead after 48 minutes through England schoolboys centre forward Stan Wynn. But in a finish which was described by *Echo* football writer Argus as 'sensational', victory was snatched from Sunderland when Manchester Boys scored two goals in the last three minutes to go into the final. The *Echo* reported that centre half Jenner had another outstanding game for Sunderland Boys. The Sunderland team was: Stoddart, Ferguson, Rooks, Wright, Jenner, Oliver, Smith, Swan, Wynn, Noble and Jubb.

SUNDERLAND AND DISTRICT
SCHOOLS' FOOTBALL ASSOCIATION.

ENGLISH SCHOOLS' TROPHY—7th ROUND.

SUNDERLAND BOYS v LIVERPOOL BOYS

ROKER PARK GROUND,

On SATURDAY, MARCH 26th, 1955

KICK-OFF 3 P.M.

SUNDERLAND BOYS
(Red and White Stripes, Black pants)

F. Stoddart
(Redby)

D. Ferguson   R. Rooks
(Castletown)   (Barnes)

B. Wright   J. Jenner   G. Oliver
(Commercial Road)   (St. Benet's R.C.)   (Bede Grammar)

B. Ward   J. Swan   S. Wynn   A. Noble   N. Jubb
(St. Aidan's R.C.) (Seaham St. Joseph R.C.) (Ryhope Grammar) (Easington) (Seaham Camden Sq.)

Sunderland Boys line up against Liverpool Boys. Liverpool had equalised in the last minute but Sunderland went up and scored from the kick-off to win the match 5-4 with the last kick of the game.

16

Jubb heads a dramatic equalizer five minutes from time in front of a packed Main Stand at Roker Park to earn a replay for Sunderland Boys against Manchester Boys in 1955.

Sunderland YOC Junior League representative team in 1956. Joe Jenner is in the back row, third from left.

SUNDERLAND EDUCATION COMMITTEE

YOUTH SERVICE SYS

This is to Certify that

J. JENNER of Ebor Boys' Club played for the
Sunderland Y.O.C. Junior Football Association against
East Northumberland Youth Association on Monday,
2nd April, 1956.

Date 2nd April, 1956.

Chairman,
Youth Committee

A Certificate awarded to Joe Jenner for representing the Sunderland YOC Junior League against East Northumberland Youth Association in 1956. Joe captained the side and the result was a 2-2 draw.

Springwell United, Sunderland Amateur League (under-21s) champions, 1954-55. Back row, left to right: Tom Jones (manager), George Scott, Bobby Phayer, Tommy Tough, Dennis Taggart, Roy Fields, Peter O'Brien, Nick Cloughton. Front row: Peter Wyness, George Harding, Allan Wyness (captain) and Norman Coleman.

Sunderland Amateur League presentation night in Wetherall's Assembly Rooms in 1955. Allan Wyness, captain of Springwell United, is surrounded by his teammates as he receives the League Championship Cup from former Sunderland AFC favourite and Darlington FC manager Bobby Gurney. The League Knock-out Cup (seen on the table) was won by Cleadon Recreation Club, who also finished runners-up in the League.

Allan Wyness (right) and his cousin Peter Wyness holding the Sunderland Amateur League Championship Cup after the presentation in Wetherall's. Allan Wyness remembers: 'I originally came from Monkwearmouth and my father, Billy Wyness, was a professional footballer with Shrewsbury and Wrexham. I was with Springwell United for three seasons. I was a defensive left half and I played alongside the centre half in a position which later became known as sweeper. Our clubhouse was situated on the field at the bottom of Thorney Close Road at Thorney Close. Our home ground was a few yards away from the clubhouse and our claim to fame was that Stan Anderson, the former Sunderland AFC skipper, played for Springwell United. At the end of the 1954-55 season I captained a Sunderland local youth team which played Essen and in July 1955 I began my two-year stint in the Army. After my
National Service I played for Dawdon Colliery Welfare in the Wearside League for two seasons but when I was 25 I got married and the wife stopped me from playing football.'

Captain of Springwell United Allan Wyness and Essen Boys captain Losch (right) exchange mementos before a challenge match on Thorney Close School ground in the latter part of the 1954-55 season. The game was part of the Essen footballers 11-day exchange visit to Sunderland. The Germans were too strong for the Sunderland Amateur League leaders winning by two goals to one in front of 2,000 spectators. Goalkeeper Dennis Taggart had an outstanding game to keep the score so close.

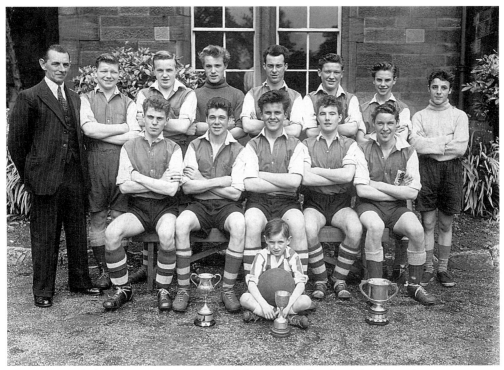

Ebor Boys Club, 1955-56. Winners of the Sunderland YOC Minor League, Captain J. Askew Memorial Cup and YOC Minor League KO Cup. Back row, left to right: Mr A. Spendley (secretary & leader), A. Edmonds, B.M. Turnbull, R. Thompson, B.W. Corbett, J. Scott, D.B. Spendley, M. Tatters. Front row: J. Robinson, R. Sumner, G.M. Tyson (captain), R. Bute and A. Robinson. The mascot is Barry Spendley.

Ebor players at the Sunderland YOC Leagues' presentation night that followed the 1955-56 season. Holding the cup is captain George Tyson who became a well-known Football League referee.

Sunderland Boys, 1957-58. Back row, left to right: Mileham (Seaham Camden Square), Farrell (St Aidan's), Ellen (West Southwick), Stephenson (Redby), Beresford (Bede), Ferry (West Park). Front row: Davison (Bede), McKinley (St Patrick's), Swan (Thompson Board), Mitchinson (Thorney Close) and Buxton (Ryhope St Patrick's). Sunderland Boys played Stoke Boys in the 6th round of the English Schools Trophy at Roker Park on Saturday 1st February 1958. Sunderland were leading 2-0 at half time but Stoke came back to win the game 3-2. Mick Buxton was manager of Sunderland AFC, 1993 to 1995.

North East Metal Fabrications (the company later became Sunderland Structural Steel), about 1959, Sunderland Amateur League champions (under-21s). Back row, left to right: Joe Jenner, Alan Wake, Jackie Clow, Ronnie Christie, Arthur Cranner, Arthur Reeves. Front row: unknown, Alf Jenner, Paddy Moran, Geordie Thompson, Geordie Kell and Frankie Pringle.

Bartram's Apprentices, 1957-58, Wearside Apprentices League winners and League Knock-out Cup runners-up. Back row, left to right: C.A. Brown (secretary), J. Hepple, K. Tansey, T. Hall, T. Rountree, J. Routledge, A. Jenner, E. Collins (chairman). Front row: J. Jenner (trainer), J.Pringle, M. Robinson, T. Bowens (captain), W. Webster, M. Charlton and L. Charles. Insets, left to right: K. Etheridge, R. Old, H. Richardson and P. Wormleighton.

Ebor Boys Club, 1958-59. Winners of the YOC Minor League, Askew Memorial Cup and League KO Cup. Back row, left to right: J. Hardy, J. Wharton, M. Gatt, J. Clark, M. Mitchell (captain), S. Collier, Mr A. Spendley (leader). Front row: T. Mitchinson, N. Richardson, C. Haley, R. Colquhoun, S. Rosebury, R. Burke and G. Armbruster. Tommy Mitchinson went on to play for Sunderland AFC.

The highly successful Sunderland YOC Junior League side, Lambton Street Boys' Club, 1968-69. Back row, left to right: Mr Alec Major (manager), Dave Preece, John Hawkins, Keith McConochie, Ken Hiles, Dave Hodgson, Jimmy Harding. Front row: John McIntosh, Tommy Dobbing (captain), Dave Hadden, Billy Palfreyman and Jimmy Roffe.

English Martyrs schoolboys Wilf Rostron (centre) and twins Tom (left) and David Callaghan were attracting Football League scouts in 1968. Their sports teacher Jack Foster said of the boys: 'I have seen the three best 11-year-old footballers of my lifetime.' Castletown lad Rostron went on to have an illustrious career with Arsenal, Sunderland and Watford between 1973 and 1983. The Callaghan twins from Marley Pots signed for Sunderland AFC but left the club in 1974. They both followed a career in the local leagues.

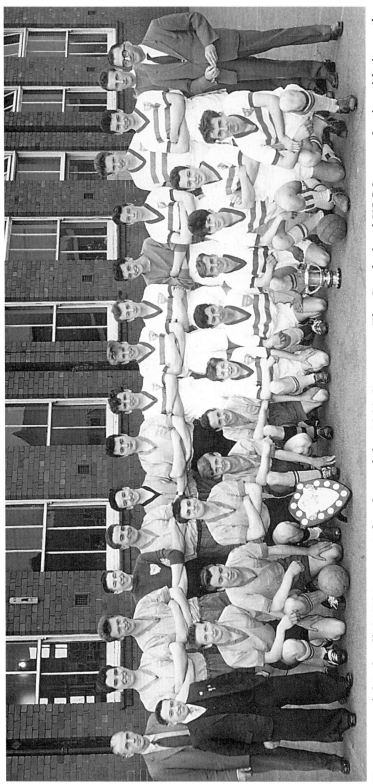

Two successful Fulwell CAYS teams at the close of the 1960-61 season. The Sunderland YOC League Junior side is on the left pictured with the McGeorge Memorial Shield and the YOC Minor League team is on the right in lighter strips with the League Championship Trophy. To be eligible to play in the YOC Junior League, players had to be less than 18 years old on 31st August. YOC Minor League players had to be under 16½ on 31st August. Fulwell CAYS Minors on the right progressed to the Junior side the following season. Their success caught the attention of Football League scouts and six of the players had trials with Newcastle United. The lads were George Liddle, Dave Craggs, Dave Hargrave, Charlie Younger, Jim Bridgewood and Gerry Donoghue (not in picture). Team manager Reg Watson was asked by an *Echo* reporter why the youngsters had been ignored by Sunderland AFC and he replied: 'It seems that you have to be Irish or Scottish to get in to Roker Park these days.'

James William Street School team in 1947. Back row, left to right: R. Pescot, S. King, T. Hull, Mr J. Barr, J. Simpson, F. Lay. Middle row: W. Gooch, W. Watson, C. Smith (captain), H. Dury, A. Rich. Front row: J. Binyon and R. Tate. Jimmy Willy's had only one side in the school and Arthur Rich, seated in the middle row at the extreme right, was only 11 years old in this 'big lads team'. Arthur went on to play for Leeds United.

St Hilda's, Division 'E' runners-up 1969-70. Back row, left to right: John Sullivan, Gary Stout, Steven Colquhoun, Chris Brown, Peter Dunningham, John Butler, Kevin Calvert. Front row: Tommy Quinn, Anthony Foster, Jimmy Mordey (captain), Chris Stewart and Peter Ross. The Junior School team scored 74 goals in 18 fixtures and Tommy Quinn got 36 of them, which included two 5's, a 4 and three hat-tricks. Chris Stewart is currently BBC's *Look North* news reporter.

Greenwell's Apprentices, 1950-51. Back row: Danny McCue (manager), Sly, Rooney, unknown, Tyler, Morrell, Weddle, unknown trainer. Front row: Newlands, Stewart, unknown, unknown and Cruikshanks.

The successful St Hilda's RC School first team, 1960-61. Back row, left to right: Kerr, Carling, Ash, Kelly, Quinn, Waggot, Smith. Front row: unknown, Fannen, Simpson, Hall (captain), Thompson, Clark and Gibson.

Bede Grammar School, League winners and Town champions, 1956-57. Back row, left to right: Mr Alan Smith, Neil Fowler, John Beresford, Fred Hodgson, Ernie Johnson, Ian Reid, John Hughes, Tom Shinkfield, Peter Cook. Front row: Wilf Harrison, Jim Davison, Alan Spedding, Stan Sampson, Gordon Clayton, Alan Simmons and Dave Snowball.

Presentation night for the YOC Leagues after the 1966-67 season in Carlton House the home of Ebor Boys' Club. The Mayor of Sunderland presents the captain of Grindon Boys' Club, Kenny Hutchinson, with the Michael Oxberry Memorial Trophy. The captains of the other successful teams look on.

Coles Cranes Juniors, 1983-84. Durham County Youth Cup winners, North East Durham Youth Cup winners, Hetton Junior League champions, Hetton Junior League Cup winners, Eye Infirmary Cup winners, Horner Cup winners and T.H. Trophy winners. Back row, left to right: Colin Pitcairn, David Revell, Ian Pattison, Kevin Wolfe, Ian Ferguson, Nigel Saddington, Gary Hunter, Joe Bittlestone, Ian Preston, John Prior, Simon Drayton and Karl Henson. Front row: Phillip James, Vincent Brand, Paul Reveley, Malcolm Scott (manager), Paul Fairweather (captain), David Edwards, William Ferry and Paul Dolan. Following Nigel Saddington's election as Sportsman of the Year and Players' Player of the Year he signed for Doncaster Rovers and later played 5 games for Sunderland before moving on to Carlisle.

Hylton Red House Primary School, winners of six trophies in the 1990-91 season, including the Durham County Primary Schools FA Cup, League Division 'B', Ditchburn Cup and Watson Cup. Back row, left to right: Stephen Haynes, David Hills, Andrew Goldsmith, Mr Smith, David Rose, Joe Davison, Craig Stafford. Front row: Stuart Hunter, Michael Butler, David Lynch, John Butler, David Simpson, Scott Jopling, Ian Mapstone and Trevor Walker, The five players in the front row on the right all played for Sunderland Boys during this successful season for the school.

St Aidan's, Durham County Schools Football Association TUC Cup winners (under-13s), 1989-90. From left to right: David Mawson, Anthony Lothian, James Taylor, Dominic Mooney, Gareth Lavender, James Robinson, David Plunkett (captain), Graham Porter, Peter Gibson Jnr, Peter Davison, Kieron Routledge, Darren Welsh and Stephen Pickering.

SECTION TWO

FOOTBALLING FAMILIES

The Robinson family from Thorney Close line up before a charity challenge match against Milton FC, Cambridge in August 1969. Mrs Bella Robinson is pictured in front of her children from the left: Joan, Eddie, Leslie, Brian, Ray, David, Ronnie, Jackie, Michael, Donny, Charlie, Robert and Miriam. Miriam is the mother of David Dolan, the 2002 Commonwealth Games super-heavyweight boxing gold medallist.

Football Family Robinson

The Robinson family of Thorney Close Estate rose to national fame in 1968 when they formed a family football team and challenged family sides throughout the country to charity matches. The eleven brothers and three sisters are the sons and daughters of former professional boxer Jack Robinson. All of the boys also took up boxing, learning the skills from their father and at Lambton Street Boys' Fellowship where they won many honours and national titles.

On Sunday morning, 18th February 1968 at Thorney Close, the Robinsons took on a team of TV personalities captained by former Newcastle United and England centre forward Jackie Milburn. Jackie is pictured with Joan (26), on the left, and Miriam (17). The girls came on as substitutes at half time to help the family win 7-2. The game was in aid of the British Olympic Fund. There were over 1,000 spectators present and highlights of the game were televised.

On Saturday morning, 17th August 1968, again at Thorney Close, the Robinsons (pictured left) played the Nevin family from Birmingham to raise money for Sunderland boys' clubs. Sunderland MP Gordon Bagier (centre) kicked off the game, which resulted in a 4-2 victory for the Robinsons.

An extract taken from the match programme when the Robinsons played Milton FC on 31st August 1969.

The Robinsons from Sunderland have set the north alight with their own special brand of 'cup-tie fever' – family football. But this is their first visit down south to play in aid of Professor Mitchell's Cancer Research Fund. In the three years they have been playing together they remain undefeated, now claiming the unofficial English family football championship after defeating a Birmingham family, the Nevins, 3-1. Up north they have earned thousands of supporters and their visit to Milton today is part of a longer programme in a bid to win the European family football title from the Germans, who have a league for this kind of competition and at present maintain they are the champions. Besides eleven brothers, there are three sisters in the Robinson family, but none of them have turned out since the competition became more serious than at the outset. They and their mother are today expected to give encouragement from the sidelines. The Robinsons have seven players with Football League experience. Their gold strip is surmounted by a specially designed family crest.

CHARITY FOOTBALL MATCH

Robinson Brothers XI
From Sunderland

versus

Milton F.C.

Sunday, 31st August 1969

K.O. 3 p.m.

Milton Recreation Ground

All Proceeds to
Professor Mitchell's Cancer Research Fund

Nº 0945   ADMISSION BY PROGRAMME 2/6

Front cover for the match programme.

Robinson Brothers

RONNIE Robinson

JACKIE Robinson   LESLIE Robinson

ROBERT Robinson DONALD Robinson DAVID Robinson

CHARLIE Robinson   EDDIE Robinson

RAY Robinson   MICHAEL Robinson   BRIAN Robinson

The Robinson brothers line-up as recorded by the match programme for the fixture against Milton FC, Cambridge on 31st August 1969.

The Robinson Trophy donated by the family to Sunderland Schools FA which is competed for each season by local primary schools.

Up and coming footballers and boxers – left to right: Robert (13), Donald (10), Charles (12), and Michael (17) Robinson in March 1958.

Boxing and football were a serious business in the Robinson household. Leslie (left) and Michael spar on the patio of their home at Tadcaster Road, about 1957, while the family looks on.

Veitchs of Pallion

Danny Veitch (*left*) played local football but his passion for boxing took over. Danny was a professional boxer who fought at fairgrounds and he would also travel to various parts of the country for £5 to £7 a fight. On 24th September 1927 Danny went 10 rounds with Jack Casey but he lost on points. *Right*: Danny Veitch Jnr, home on leave in 1949, is pictured with his brother George who was playing for Silksworth CW Juniors. George went on to play for Millwall, 1952-57.

The Conlons

A family affair. Seven members of the Conlon family are in this photograph of Dagmar FC taken during the 1989-90 season. Back row, left to right: Ted Wooton, Peter Boyle, Tony Braid, Eddie Brown, Shaun Todd, Peter Gibson, Paul Tench, Brian Conlon, Ian Freeman, Dickie Conlon with son Michael. Front: Keith Cullen, Tommy Ewart, Leighan Conlon, Sid Conlon, Ken Dugdale, Davie Conlon and Davie Stobbart.

Davie Conlon, a temperamental but highly skilful right winger who was often among the goals, in action in March 1982.

Keen, confident and up for it. Sid Conlon with his boots under his arm on his way to Marley Pots to play for the Dagmar in the late 1980s.

Although some managers did not share Sid's belief in his own ability none of them can deny his enthusiasm and passion for the game. And, as can be clearly seen from the photograph, injuries did not deter Sid from playing.

Four Generations of the Edwards Family

Football in the Edwards family can be traced back for four generations. Thomas Edwards played in goal for Dawdon CW in the 1930s and his son Peter was selected to play for Sunderland Boys in 1959. His teammate was Jimmy Montgomery. Left half Peter played for many years in the Sunderland & District

Arthur Bond, maternal grandfather of David, Mark and Peter Edwards, in his playing days for Pallion Junior School in 1932.

League and he was a member of the Grange United treble-winning side of 1976. Peter had three sons – David, Mark and Peter Jnr. Their maternal grandfather Arthur Bond played at outside left in the local leagues and he had trials with Derby County towards the end of the war. With this strong family football background the Edwards brothers reached a high standard in non-league football. The eldest brother David, a left-sided midfielder, played for Hayes and Borehamwood in the Vaux Opel League in 1985, and he had trials with Ipswich Town and Sheffield United. Mark and Peter Jnr both signed apprentice forms for Berwick Rangers in 1989 and they turned out for the reserves. In 1990 outside left Mark played for Shildon in the Northern League and in 1991 left sided midfielder Peter Jnr turned out for Northern League outfit Ryhope CA. Although the three bothers have finished playing the cycle continues with Mark's son, 9-year-old Louis, turning out for Redby CA at left back in a small-sided boys' league.

Thomas Edwards, goalkeeper for Dawdon CW in 1937.

Pallion Junior School, 1953-54. Back row, left to right: Graham Defty, Harry Patterson, Melvin Nash, George Virtue, John Patterson, Fred Leck. Front row: Tommy Reay, David Snowball, PETER EDWARDS (captain), Wilf Harrison and David Bambrough.

Town End Junior School in 1976. Back row, left to right: John Dixon, David Pullan, Ian Hall, Alan Eden, Mr Malcolm Young (teacher), Steven Hopper, Paul Robson, Thomas England. Middle row: Darren Kemp, Steven Curtis, DAVID EDWARDS, Billy Fisher, Keith Dimmock, Eric Allan. Front row: David Hair, Tony Miller, Graeme Nicholson and Kevin Cleugh.

Mark Edwards, Seaburn Dene Juniors, 1983.

Peter Edwards Jnr, Seaburn Dene Juniors, 1984.

Louis Edwards, Redby CA Under-8s, 2001.

Jim, Bob and Alan Davison

The Davison brothers were born in Tower Street, Hendon, the same street where Raich Carter was born. The brothers attended Hendon Board School and they all played for the school team and represented Sunderland Juniors (under-11s) at football. The sportsmaster at Hendon Board School, Mr Liddle, made a lasting impression on the boys, being an excellent coach at both football and cricket. Jim Davison passed his 11-plus for the Bede and on leaving school he came through the Sunderland youth system with Silksworth Juniors and signed for Sunderland Football Club.

Jimmy Davison aged 18 (partially hidden by the post) scores his first goal for Sunderland against Luton Town at Roker Park on New Year's Eve, 1960.

Jimmy Davison in Bolton Wanderers colours. Jim made 72 appearances for Sunderland between November 1959 and November 1963 and he scored 11 goals. His first game for the club was when he had just turned 17. Jimmy transferred to Bolton and then to Queen of the South in 1965. Jim was a qualified chartered accountant and he returned to this work when his football career ended. Jim Davison died suddenly in February 1987 at the age of 44.

Jimmy Davison (left) and the legendary Jim Montgomery in Trafalgar Square about 1960. The teammates were on their way to an international youth tournament with Sunderland AFC.

Sunderland Juniors wearing Arsenal strips in 1959. Notice the junior bar attached to the goal. Bob Davison is pictured front row on the extreme left.

Bob (left) and Alan Davison at a wedding at St Ignatious Church in 1974. Bob represented Sunderland Boys and Durham County Boys at cricket at under-15 level. He also played for Ivy Leaf Cricket Club in the Wearside League.

Mr Liddle, Hendon Board School sportsmaster, who encouraged and coached the Davison brothers at both football and cricket.

The Gibbon Brothers

Billy Gibbon (born 1951), manager of Hepworth and Grandage SC for six seasons in the 1980s. Billy is remembered for his aggressive team talks to lift his players before games and at half time.

Tommy Gibbon (born 1949), the eldest of the Gibbon brothers. He played in goal at school and afterwards as a left back. He loved Thistle FC and when he retired from playing he supported the team and his two younger brothers, Tony and Chipper. Tommy is well

remembered and appreciated for the hard work he put in to rub down the legs of the players on cold mornings before a game. He used to be soaking with sweat. None of the lads begrudged his valiant attempts to replace the liquid in the Thistle Club after the game.

Tony Gibbon (born 1952), centre forward and prolific goal scorer for Thistle FC from 1976 to 1982.

Bobby Gibbon (born 1957), centre half for Thistle FC and captain of Hepworth & Grandage SC. Known as 'Chipper', not a tall lad but good in the air and he timed his headers well.

The Five Burke Brothers

Four of the Burke brothers line up in the Red House WMC side of the mid 1960s. Back row, second from the left is striker Kevin. Front row, extreme left is Bobby. On the end right is Terry. Next to Terry is Paddy who was a powerfully built goal scoring centre forward and a tough competitor. The brothers are perhaps best remembered for their playing days at Downhill WMC. Managed by Terry Burke they were a dominant force in the Sunderland Sunday League during the 1970s. Inset: Youngest of the footballing brothers, John Burke, in his playing days with the Transport Club, 1980-81.

Like Father Like Son

William Henry, centre forward and captain of Sunderland East End's championship-winning team St John's Church Institute in 1927, which played in the Church Institute League.

Kit Henry, William's son, leading goal scorer for East End CA in the late 1950s and early '60s. Kit is remembered as a rough, old-fashioned centre forward who knocked defenders about.

The Howey Family

Havelock Secondary Modern first team, 1959-60. Back row, left to right: Avery, McQuillan, Fearn, NORMAN HOWEY, Keethley, Thompson, Marshall, Kilbey. Front row: Mr Bell, Hickey, Smith, Wainwright (captain), MacDonald and Skaug.

Norman Howey, father of the footballing brothers Lee and Steve, played for Herrington CW Juniors in the Hetton Junior League before progressing to Herrington CW in the Wearside League. From about 1965 to 1973 Norman also turned out for Wearside League sides Hylton CW, Silksworth CW and Whitburn. He also played in the competitive Sunderland CIU League for Farringdon Club. Norman was an old fashioned centre forward who liked scoring goals and he recalls a memorable weekend during his playing career:

'Football was a lot more physical in those days and centre halves got away with murder. One Saturday afternoon I was playing for Whitburn against Gateshead in the FA Cup at the Redheugh Stadium. The ball was at the other end of the pitch when the centre half punched me in the back of the head. I retaliated and we were both sent off for fighting. The next day I was captain for Farringdon Club against South Hylton Club and there was a bit of animosity between the opposing players and supporters. I had a run-in with their centre half and I was sent off again, and so was he.' Norman continued playing in Sunday football until he was 37 when he retired to concentrate on following the progress of his two sons, Lee and Steve, who were showing great promise in the Sunderland Schools' League.

Norman Howey (right) with teammate Tommy Conroy, the well known boxing promoter, during their playing days for Whitburn FC in 1970.

Sunderland Boys Primary Schools squad in about 1980. Lee Howey is standing to the left of the boy on shoulders. Football League referees George Tyson is on the right and Pat Partridge is on the left behind Lee.

Norman Howey recalls: 'When we lived at Gilley Law in about 1977 our Lee was about 8 and Steven 6. There was a patch of grass outside of our flat where the boys would go for a kick-about with some older lads. The big lads would put our Steven in goal because he was the youngest. That little patch of grass was certainly a hotbed of budding professional footballers because among those boys involved in the kick-abouts were Mick Hazard (Spurs) and Kevin Dillon (Newcastle and Birmingham) who lived over the road to us, and Mick Smith who lived in our building. Mick progressed through the leagues from the 4th to the old 1st Division with Wimbledon.'

Below centre: Proud dad Norman with sons Steven (14) and Ipswich Town Youth team player Lee (16). The occasion was when Steven signed associate schoolboy forms with Newcastle United during the summer of 1986.

Football continues in the Howey family with Lee's son Elliot (6) on the left who looks forward to his football coaching sessions on Saturday mornings. Steven's son Jed (3) on the right is wearing his dad's team's strip – Manchester City.

Brothers Lee Howey, the Sunderland utility player and Steven (front), the Newcastle United central defender, are pictured as friendly rivals in 1993. Their father Norman remembers: 'When Lee and Steven were boys I used take them on to a spare field to train them to master the basic skills with no fancy stuff. They practised controlling the ball and finding a player and it was rewarding seeing them using their skills for St Cuthbert's School team. At that early age I could see they had potential and natural talent and I supported and encouraged them. The boys were centre forwards at school and they were outstanding. They scored goals by the boatload for St Cuthbert's, St Aidan's and Sunderland Boys. During the 1982-83 season St Cuthbert's scored 198 goals and our Steven got 125 of them. During the same season our Lee was playing in a game for St Aidan's against Southmoor when he scored all ten goals in a 10-2 win. The boys were always strikers and I would never have dreamt they

would both be converted to central defenders during their professional careers. I'm extremely proud of Lee and Steven. Their sons, Elliot and Jed, are football daft and I can see at their early age that my grandsons have potential.'

Steve Howey rises above the Portuguese defence to power in a header for England at Wembley on 12th December 1995. England drew the game 1-1 and Steve was marking the brilliant Figo. Looking on are Les Ferdinand and Paul Gascoigne on the left. Steve Howey won four England caps from 1994 to 1996 and his dad Norman recalls that his son would have won more had it not been for some serious injuries.

Jenner Brothers

Joe and Alfie Jenner were both central defenders but when they played together in the same team Alf, the younger brother by one year, reverted to full back. The brothers played together for North East Met Fab, Thorney Close WMC and Farringdon FC. Joe and Alf were employed as shipwrights at JL Thompson's shipyard.

Above: Joe Jenner in Sunderland Boys colours, 1954-55. Joe is also pictured with his school team St Benet's in 1955 in the back row extreme right. In 1963 the Jenner brothers played for Thorney Close WMC in the Sunderland & District League and both were reported to have had an outstanding game against the strong Pyrex side at South Hylton. Thorney were losing 0-2 at half-time but won the game 4-2. Their skipper Peter Wyness also had an excellent game and the goal scorers were Tom Tough and Roy Fields. Alf remembers that Roy Fields was the best centre forward he ever played with.

Above: Alfie Jenner in his playing days for the successful Bartram's Apprentices during the 1957-58 season. A good header of the ball, Alfie was also a strong, hard-tackling defender who, it was said, took no prisoners. Brian Clough presented Alfie, as captain of Thorney Close WMC, with the Leukemia Cup in 1963. Alfie remembers that Clough, with usual bluntness, told him to go and get his haircut!

The Callaghans

Tommy Callaghan Snr was well known in football circles around the town. He had a broad knowledge of the game as a player, referee and manager. In 1953 he began his National Service as an 18-year-old. Tommy continued with his football career in the Army but broke his leg in two places. There were complications and Tommy spent the last year of his two-year conscription in a military hospital. After leaving the Army he returned to Joplings Steel Foundry where he worked and played football for them. Tommy played for the strong Southwick St Hilda's side of the late 1950s. But he wasn't a Catholic and despite being a regular player he was barred from playing for St Hilda's in the Durham County Catholic Cup. That disappointed him

Tommy Callaghan 1935-1989.

remembers his widow Vera. Teammate Barney Sanderson remembers: 'I can recall the days of the heavy leather ball. I was only a little lad and on wet heavy grounds the ball soaked in water like a sponge. I found it difficult to shoot in those conditions. But Tommy Callaghan was a well-built man and he packed a tremendous shot in even the heaviest of conditions.'

In the mid 1960s Tommy took up refereeing. He had high standards and he was a fair man. He had firm control of hard games and consequently he gained the respect of players. Tommy was an influential character with Thistle FC in the late 1970s and early '80s and he had a guiding fatherly influence on the players. Left winger Jessie Cresswell recalls: 'I can remember well Tommy's team talks before a big game. He would gain the attention of the players and then pause while he lit up his pipe. He gave us that little bit extra confidence and belief in ourselves'. And, centre forward Tony Gibbon recalls: 'Tommy was inspirational. In the 1981-82 season we reached the final of the Boldon Charity Cup. Tommy pulled me to one side before the game and said: "The biggest and hardest task in football is scoring goals. We are all relying on you today Tony." We went out and beat Gael Golden Lion 4-0 and I scored all four goals.'

Tom and Vera Callaghan had twin boys, Thomas and David, born in 1956. The twins were naturally introduced to football at an early age and Football League scouts soon noticed the talent they displayed for their school team and for Sunderland Boys. The twins signed for Sunderland AFC and played for the youth team. Tom and Dave left Sunderland AFC in 1974 and they became well-known in North East football leagues.

David Callaghan (white shorts) in action for Sunderland Boys against Newcastle Boys at Roker Park during the 1970-71 season.

Thomas (left) and David Callaghan meet Stoke City footballers Gordon Banks and George Eastham before the Sunderland versus Stoke, First Division game on 1st March 1969.

Seeing Double

Vera Callaghan remembers how easy it was to get Thomas and David confused: 'Once you get to know the twins you can tell the difference but other people cannot. On one occasion, when they were both playing for Humbledon Plains Farm WMC, Thomas got booked. He was regularly booked but David was rarely in trouble. Thomas was on two bookings and a third would mean a suspension so he told the referee he was David Callaghan. The ref asked if he was sure, and then David's name went into the book. After the game Thomas asked Dave if it was all right. 'It will have to be. It's too late now,' said Dave. There was another occasion when they played for the school cricket team. David was a good batsman and our Tom was further down the order. During a game Dave and the early order batsmen were out and things were looking bad for the team, so our David went in to bat again instead of our Tom. That was a bit naughty.'

David and Thomas Callaghan in September 1992.

Vera Callaghan, secretary of Torrens FC in the 1970s.

Vera recalls a brainwave from Tommy: 'Before the days of nets referees had difficulty judging whether a shot had passed either side of the post and many arguments and trouble was caused by goals being allowed when the ball had gone for a goal kick, and the reverse of course. Tommy solved the problem by taking our twins with him to games he refereed and placed one behind each goal. If Tommy had any doubt about a shot he would look to one of our lads who would signal a goal by a thumbs up. The twins were reluctant to go with their dad at first until Tommy told them he would give each half-a-crown out of the 15 shillings referee's fee.'

Right: John Scott, brother to Vera and the twins' uncle. Scotty was a strong tackling defender and a good leader. He was captain of Thistle FC from 1976 to 1980. John was Player of the Year for the Thistle in 1980.

Below: Sunderland AFC player Dave Watson presents Paul Scrafton captain of Roker Boys' Club with the Sunderland YOC League under-15s Championship Trophy in 1971. The group of happy lads includes Tom and Dave Callaghan. It is interesting to point out that current Sunderland AFC player, Michael Proctor, is a second cousin to the Callaghan twins.

SECTION THREE

CUP FINALS AND CHAMPIONS

One of the Paxton brothers of Universal Sealant Limited, sponsors of the outstanding Sunderland CIU League side Humbledon Plains Farm, presents club captain Alan Laws with one of the strips the team will wear in the final of the All-England FA Sunday Cup Final at St James' Park on 1st May 1988.

Hood Street Methodists

In February 1950 Hood Street Brotherhood FC were bottom of the Wearside Combination League's third division. The club made new signings; they won promotion to the second division and they built a team that was to put in a serious challenge for the All-Britain Methodist Cup, a prestigious competition in those days. In February 1954 the Street defeated Simonside Methodists from Newcastle 3-2 after extra time in a third round tie. Captain Harry Holt played an inspirational game with Moffat and Mudd among the goals. New signing Jimmy Maughan settled in well at left back and in March 1954 the Street took on and beat Greenhill Methodists from Sheffield in the semi-final. Hood Street's ambition to lift the trophy caught the imagination of football clubs in Sunderland. Wearmouth CW offered their ground as a training facility where the Hood Street players improved their fitness. Even Sunderland Football Club chipped in and loaned the team a set of red and white strips for Hood Street to represent the town in the final. Nottingham Forest hosted the final tie on Saturday 24th April 1954. Their opponents East Hill from Dartford in Kent had won the trophy once and this was their fourth final. The match kicked-off at 6 pm and East Hill went ahead after five minutes. Hood Street played well in the first half with right back Murdy outstanding. Wilson equalized for Hood Street and that is how it stood at half time. The Wearsiders were forced to defend for most of the second half and the more experienced East Hill triumphed by five goals to one. The defeat was a bitter blow to Hood Street but the following season, 1954-55, saw the Street on the All-Britain Methodist Cup trail again but they were beaten in the semi-final 5-2. However, they say that God loves a trier and 1959-60 was to be Hood Street's season. Goalscoring machine, Roy Fields, played a large part in the Street's passage to the final which took place on St Alban's ground, Hertfordshire and where the Wearside Combination division one side hammered Abbey Wood from Kent 5-2. Defender Tom Bewick remembers: 'The Abbey Wood players were a good set of lads and they took the defeat well. Both teams took part in the after match celebrations in a local pub where one of their player's asked what we trained on up in Sunderland because we were so fit. "Just beer and raw meat", was the reply.'

A cartoon from the *Football Echo*, 22nd November 1952.

Hood Street Methodists pictured at King George V playing fields with the All-Britain Methodist Cup. Back row, left to right: Mr Jones, John Hudson (manager), Peter Elliot, Tom Bewick, Jimmy Green, Gordon Jones, Robert Miller, Dennis Pearn, Peter Herd, William Peterson, George Thompson, 'Archie' the physiotherapist. Front row: George Daley, Arthur Reeves, Dempsey Leonard, Roy Fields and Alan Wilson.

Right: Hood Street Methodists players and supporters in Trafalgar Square before the All-Britain Methodist Cup final towards the end of the 1959-60 season. Back row, left to right: Jackie Clow, Tom Bewick, Peter Herd, Arthur Reeves, Alan Wilson. Front row: Geordie Thompson, supporter, Andy Christie, Robbo Miller and Roy Fields.

The successful Hetton CIU League side Pallion Workmen's Club of the late 1960s. Seated behind the cup is centre half and captain Arthur Rich. Arthur recalls that Pallion were the only Sunderland team in the league at the time. Then Southwick and the Boilermakers entered. Every game was like a cup final, remembers Arthur, because of the rivalry with the colliery teams. They all wanted to beat 'the townies'.

Torrens FC, winners of the Sunderland Sunday League Division 2 in 1971-72 season without dropping a point. Back row, left to right: B. Goldsmith, T. Callaghan, A. Boxer, A. Goldsmith, B. Harrison, G. Hounslow, P. Clark, J. Flett, J. Gibson, A. Goldsmith, A. Miller, J. McGuire, A. Dagg, P. Peterson, N. Brown Jnr. (manager), N. Brown Snr. Front row: V. Callaghan, K. Smiles, J. Scott, J. Higgins, T. Clark (captain), G. Smith, W. Robson, M. Clark and G. Hall.

Howard's FC, winners of the Wearside Combination League Cup, the Alan Hood Memorial Trophy and the Wearmouth and Hylton Aged Miners' Cup, 1997-98. Back row, left to right: Anthony Pemberton, Mark Pemberton, Nicky Pemberton (player manager), Stan James, Darren Watson, Dave Stobbart, Chris Campbell, Lee Ellison, David Pringle, Glen Connelly, Peter Wright, Jeff Smith, Jonty Pemberton (captain). Front row: Tony Humble, Paul Pemberton, Dave Downing, Ken Dugdale and Peter Humble. Insets: left to right, Paul Tench, Julian Cliff, Steven Burnett and Sid Mordey.

Right: Jonty Pemberton, captain of Howard's FC, displays the Alan Hood Memorial Trophy in 1998.

Pioneers of Sunday Football

It is hard to believe today but for many years organised football on Sundays was banned in this country. However, after the Second World War there were moves afoot to have Sunday football officially recognised, which the Football Association strenuously resisted.

By 1950 Durham FA were supporting the Football Association's stand to keep the Sabbath day. The traditionalists also argued that the game in this country would change as we know it because of the popularity of football with players and spectators and many clubs might prefer to change over to play on Sundays instead of Saturdays which would upset the league programme. However, the advocators of Sunday football said that Sunday was the only day that many men and youths were available to play football owing to work commitments; and that other sports were permitted on Sundays and therefore football should not be banned. Durham FA was watching the situation closely and in an attempt to curb the advancement of football on Sundays they made warnings to players and to referees with threats of suspensions if they were discovered taking part in organised matches. The word organised was defined as: 'competitive and under the jurisdiction of a league committee.'

In March 1950 *Football Echo* writer W.S. Turnbull called for the FA never to relax their rule which banned Sunday football and he argued: 'I cannot imagine unaffiliated football ever being a success if experienced men will hold themselves aloof from it.' Nonetheless the advocators of Sunday football were persistent in their attempts to persuade the FA to officially recognise football on the Sabbath. However, despite the threats unaffiliated games were taking place and as a consequence referees were suspended and some had their certificates cancelled as a result of defying the FA directive. In Sunderland a group of Sunday football enthusiasts led by Gordon Howe met in the Station Hotel and the Wellington Tavern in Southwick and they formed an unaffiliated Sunderland Sunday Football League in 1958. Gordon recalls: 'The lads I can remember who helped me to set up the league included Billy Bell, Jimmy Wilson and little Frankie Davis. We knew that an organised league was

Founder of the unaffiliated Sunderland Sunday League, Gordon Howe (right), presents Wellington Tavern player Jimmy Christie with his league winners' trophy in 1959.

Gordon Howe (left) and Billy Bell, hold the League championship trophy at the first presentation night of the unaffiliated Sunderland Sunday League in the Station Hotel, Southwick in 1959.

prohibited but we got round that by calling them all friendlies. It was a league among ourselves and we just went on to the local pitches on Sunday mornings and we played football for nowt. We didn't pay any rent for the pitches. There were about eight teams in the league, which included Webster Davison, Reeds the printers, Smythes the bakers, Farm Stores and the Wellington Tavern. All of the clubs pooled money for the league championship trophy and I went to buy it at Walkers in the town centre.'

Sunday Leagues like the one in Sunderland were springing up all over the country and pressure was mounting on the Football Association to recognise the inevitable, and during the close season of 1960 the FA wrote to all County FAs: 'County Associations may now invite Sunday leagues and clubs in their County to affiliate to their association if they wish to accept them.' County FAs were given the choice whether or not to recognise the Sunday leagues operating within their jurisdiction. Durham Football Association was one of several County FAs throughout the country which decided not to break with tradition and to keep the Sabbath day. Once again instructions were issued to players and referees in County Durham to refrain from involvement in Sunday football. Durham FA stated that they would discipline offenders like the referee who was discovered officiating in a local Sunday league game. However, Durham Football Association finally relented and Sunday football leagues in County Durham were finally affiliated and the official Sunderland Sunday League came in to being in 1963.

Despite the country's governing body originally making it clear that they had no intention of organising Sunday football they embraced the new culture and introduced a national competition in 1964 – The Football Association Sunday Cup. The Sunday football pioneers efforts had been rewarded and justified despite the old fashioned traditional views. By 1990, 40,000 Sunday league clubs were registered with the Football Association.

All Left-Footers

Barney Sanderson recalls: 'I began my National Service in the Army in 1954 when I was 21. I became super-fit with the Army training and I played for the regiment all over Germany. When I was on leave I played a game for St Hilda's and I found that I was yards faster than the others. I played in a pair of light low cut continental boots with moulded studs, which were popular in Germany. The lads here were still wearing the heavy leather boots with leather studs secured with nails. I enjoyed showing off my new style boots. It was a bit of a novelty because the lads hadn't seen them before. When I left the Army in 1956 I signed on for St Hilda's in the Sunderland & District League. You had to be a Catholic to play for them. In the 1958-59 season we won the Durham Minor Cup, the Durham Catholic Cup and the league. We were the first Sunderland team to win the Durham Minor Cup and teams from higher leagues began poaching our players. Arthur Boxer, for example, signed professional forms for South Shields. The team finally folded in 1961 and I signed for Sunderland West End in the Wearside Combination League. Their home ground was at King George V Playing Fields and I played for them until 1965. West End was a dominant force in the town and when we turned out we didn't expect to lose. I

Barney Sanderson in his Army playing days.

can remember a few members of the Donkin family playing for West End over the years. We went for the Durham Minor Cup but could only reach the semis.'

Presentation night in Pennywell Workmen's Club for the successful Sunderland West End side at the end of the 1961-62 season. Captain and right half Jimmy Ramsey is presented with the Seaham Aged Miners' Cup. West End were also Wearside Combination League Division 1 champions and Knock-out Cup winners. Barney Sanderson recalls that about two years later Jimmy Ramsey was killed in an accident at Bartram's shipyard.

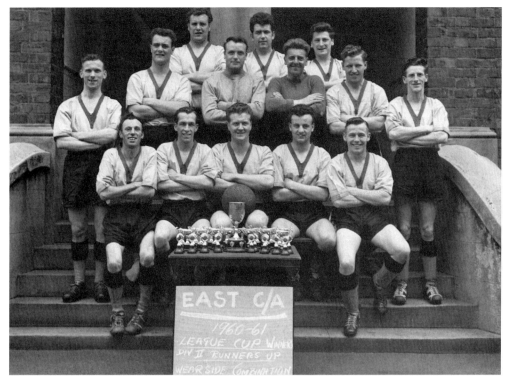

Sunderland East End Community Association, Wearside Combination League Cup winners and Division 2 runners-up, 1960-61. Back row, left to right: Kit Henry, Tommy Cruikshanks, Gerry Watson. Middle row: John Truman, Tommy Blanchard, Charlie Moore, Larry McCue, ? Graham, Ernie Dawson. Front row: Billy Snowball, Alan Ward, Sid Swales (captain), Terry Waugh and Alan Smith. The photograph was taken on the steps of the former Sunderland Orphanage building which housed the community association.

Sunderland East End CA presentation night in the old Orphanage, June 1961.

East End CA centre forward Kit Henry receives his individual trophy from the manager of Timpson's shoe shop on 15th June 1961. Timpson's were the sponsors of the League Knock-out Cup.

Grange United, managed by Sid Walton pictured sitting on extreme left, were Sunderland & District League treble winners, 1975-76. The trophies are from left to right: Leukemia Cup, Ken Atkinson Memorial Trophy and League Championship Trophy.

Sunderland Fire Service, North East Inter-Fire Service Trophy winners in 1973. Back row, left to right: Tom Callaghan (referee) George Irwing, Ron Bosher, Trevor Whitehead, Paddy Moran, John Martin, Dick Bull, Wilf Tindale, Fred Crawford. Front row: Stan Carr, Peter Ould, Les Davison, David Moon and Tommy Barnes. Sunderland beat Cleveland 8-3 in the final. All of the players were Sunderland men. In 1974 Sunderland Fire Service was absorbed by Tyne & Wear Metropolitan Fire Service and Dick Bull is currently Chief Fire Officer.

Thorney Close WMC, winners of the Sunderland & District League, the Leukemia Cup and the League Knock-out Cup, 1963. Back row, left to right: Dickie King (secretary), Ron Robinson, Sid Walker, unknown committee man, Charlie Watt (trainer), Dennis Taggart, Terry Burke, Topper Jones (committee man). Front row: Joe Jenner, John 'Wily' Thompson, Bobby Robinson, Roy Fields, Mickey Robinson, Alfie Jenner (captain) and Billy Lister.

Hendon Sports Club, 1950-51. Unbeaten Wearside Combination League Division 2 champions and League Cup winners. Players named only. Back row, left to right: Willie Snowball, Ralphy Hill, Jimmy Herron. Middle row: Geordie Davison, Dennis Colquhoun, Ron Knowles, Billy Stokell. Front row: Dick Wilson, Eddie Taylor, Eddie Johnson, Alec Russell, Fred Hutchinson, Roy Turner, Ralphy Hales and Tommy Davies. Huge crowds would assemble on Hendon Burn to watch this successful young side. Dennis Colquhoun scored 76 league and cup goals during the 1950-51 season.

Ken Atkinson Memorial Trophy winners Joplings in 1976.

Farringdon FC, 1963-64, the undefeated Sunderland & District League champions, Leukemia Cup and League Challenge Cup winners. Back row, left to right: Jackie Cook, Kenny Bainbridge, Billy Cuthbertson, Bobby Markham, Wily Thompson, Billy Chalk, Alf Jenner, Clem Ferry, Ted the trainer, Billy Graham. Front row: Billy Turnbull, Tommy Tough, Dave Riddell, Billy Punchon and Sid Walker.

Former Sunderland and England right half Stan Anderson presents Farringdon FC captain Alfie Jenner with his individual trophy at the Sunderland & District presentation night in 1964.

Sunderland GPO

Sunderland General Post Office FC played in the Sunderland Wednesday League. One of their players was Bob Gibson who played for them for 13 years between 1957 and 1970. Bob recalls: 'I was 16 years old when I first played for the GPO. The sides in the league in those days included Sunderland Butchers, Ryhope Co-op, Sunderland Police, Sunderland Fire Brigade, Northern Buses and Corporation Buses. Our home pitch was Wearmouth Colliery Welfare and the Post Office would give us a couple of hours or so off work to play football. The big game in the years that I played for the GPO was the Durham County Wednesday League's Cup final at Ferens Park, Durham City in about 1967 when we defeated Darlington Police two nil. By the early 1970s the Sunderland Wednesday League was in decline. The traditional half-day closing on Wednesday was dying out and the lads couldn't get the time off work like they used to do. The league folded in about 1974.'

Right: A cartoon from the *Football Echo*, 14th February 1953.

Sunderland GPO in about 1970. Back row, left to right: John Whitehouse (Postmaster of Sunderland), Bob Gibson, Taffy Thomas, Arthur Harkness, Joe Harrison, John Harkness, Peter Hill, Stan Scott, Walter Head, Gordon McDonald (manager), Steve Brettel. Front row: Ralphy Herrington, Les Turner, unknown, Larry McGuinness and Andy Wyness. The trophies include the Sunderland Wednesday League Championship Cup (centre).

The jubilant North Star players and supporters after beating Hylton Lodge 4-1 in the KO Cup final on their home pitch at Hylton Colliery Welfare in May 1976. Hylton Lodge were the unbeaten Wearside Combination League champions and Peter Gibson remembers: 'As soon as the final whistle blew Hylton Lodge's manager Peter Phillipson was the first on to the pitch to shake the North Star  players' hands to congratulate us. I thought that was really big of him.' The North Star went on to win the KO Cup four seasons in succession.

Hylton Lodge FC, unbeaten Wearside Combination League champions, 1976-77. Back row, left to right: P. Phillipson (manager), A. Bell, C. Betts, J. Wood, J Owens, G. Raine (captain), B. Davison, G. Wardle, D. Raine (secretary). Front row: A. Stokoe, D. Hartley, E. Henderson, A. Rushworth, L. Sheriff and D. Elliot. Mascot: Alan Sheriff.

Southwick Football Club, 1954-55. Unbeaten Sunderland & District League champions, and winners of the League Cup, the Wearmouth & Hylton Aged Miners' Cup and the Oddfellows Cup. They also reached the semi-final of the prestigious Durham Minor Cup. Back row, left to right: Andra Clark, Chris Hall, Jimmy Robinson, Dennis Colquhoun, Doug Hall, Cec Crosbie. Front row: Tom Leadbitter, Dennis Philliskirk, John Carter, Geordie Calvert and Gordon Drinkald. The mascot is Tommy Clark.

Lee Butler, captain of Jacksons, Monkwearmouth, holds aloft the Wearside Combination League Challenge Cup in May 2001 after their 4-0 victory over Gideons in the final.

Thorney Close Youth Club FC, 1972-73. National Under-21 Cup winners, Durham Area Under-21 champions, Sunderland & District League champions, League KO Cup winners. Back row, left to right: Ted Oliver (assistant manager), John Dickman, Chris Aitchison, Robbie Hall, Mickey Waller, Dave Steele, Joe Sherriff, Tommy Conroy, Tommy Hammond, Brian Davison, Tony Green (manager). Front row: Trevor Hollingshead, Bobby McKenzie, Robbie Maw, Paul Graham, Davy Jones, Tommy Dobbing, George Spurs and Mickey Graham. Inset: Barry Dunn became a professional footballer with Sunderland AFC in September 1979 at the age of 27. Barry made 25 appearances for Sunderland and scored 2 goals.

Grindon Mill, Sunderland & District League winners, 1974-75. Captain Mid Royal holds the Championship Trophy. Standing, left to right: Mickey Reeves, Stan Lyndsey (assistant manager), Kevin Cook, Ash Spooner, Dave Ferry, Les West, John Scott, Harry Ridley, Mickey Taylor (manager). Front row: Ken Hutchinson, Alf Britton, Owen Williamson, Jimmy Rolfe and Brian Sinclair.

Hepworth & Grandage, Wearside Combination League side of 1980-81. Back row, left to right: Billy Gibbon (manager), Arthur Wardle, Neil Stafford, unknown, Dave Rose, Jessie Cresswell, Tony Gibbon, three supporters, extreme right Charlie Blyth (secretary). Front row: Derek King, Ian Kerr, Paul Davison, Kevin O'Connor, Bobby Gibbon with son Ian, Nicky Pemberton and Kevin Ross.

Hepworth & Grandage presentation night in 1982. The Wearside Combination League side were League champions, winners of the Jim Pears Memorial Trophy and the First Division Knock-out Cup.

Thistle FC, Sunderland Sunday League Division 3 champions, 1979-80. Back row, left to right: Tom Gibbon, John Milligan (manager), Alan Jackson, George Barron, Kevin Dickinson, Arthur Milligan, Mickey Campbell, Paul Davison, John Hounslow (treasurer), Charlie Robson. Front row: Peter Gibson, Robert Gibbon, Tony Gibbon, John Scott (captain), Tom Callaghan, Jessie Cresswell and Kevin Ross. Inset: Gordon Carty.

Charlie Robson (left) and Kevin O'Connor after a Bank Holiday challenge match between Thistle FC and an over-40s eleven at Marley Pots in the early 1980s.

Ray Moon, a well known footballer in Sunderland who captained Seaham Red Star, recalls: 'Charlie Robson was a real character. We both played for Laing's apprentices in the late 1960s. Billy Quarry was our captain and one Saturday morning Charlie asked Billy if he could be captain for the day because his girlfriend was coming to watch him. You know, to impress her. Billy agreed and we all played along with it. Charlie was in his element telling us all what to do and we were all replying: "Aye skipper" and "What should I do now skipper". But Charlie was deliberately going over the top and by the end of the game we were all sick of him. We couldn't wait to get him into the changing rooms where we all belted in to him, but Charlie couldn't stop laughing.'

The Football Association Sunday Cup

Humbledon Plains Farm line up before the final of the All-England FA Sunday Cup at St James' Park on 1st May 1988. Back row left to right: John Dickman Jnr, John Dickman Snr (manager), George Cook (assistant manager), Kenny Mitchell, Paul Walker, Kevin Todd, Colin Cowans, Bobby Strong, Alan Farquar, Keith Robertson, Paul Elliot, Kevin Berry, David Scott, Alan Laws. Front: Tony Maggiore, Steven Cook (mascot), David Callaghan, Brian Jennings and Thomas Callaghan. Kevin Todd and Kenny Mitchell had made a return to St James' Park where they had been professionals with Newcastle United. Plainsy went down 0-2 to Nexday from Northampton. England manager Bobby Robson was the chief guest and he presented the cup and medals to the players. However, Humbledon Plains Farm reached the FA Sunday Cup final again on 6th May 1990 when they lifted the trophy by beating Marston Sports of Wolverhampton at The Hawthorns by 2-1 to bring the cup to Sunderland for the first time. The cup winning squad was: Nigel Stewart, Tony Clark, Dave Merritt, Tony Maggiore, David Callaghan, Derek Holden, David Scott, Kenny Mitchell, Colin Shanks, Paul Walker, Darren Melville, Derek Ord, Alan Laws, Colin Watson, Neil Hixon, Keith Robertson, Paul Elliot, Paul Graham, Colin Cowans, David Hardy, John Dickman (manager), George Cook (assistant manager) and Teddy Collinson (trainer).

The North Star line up at Ryhope before the final of the Wearside Combination League Knock-out Cup in 1980. Back row, left to right: Colin Hopper, Kevin Chisholm, John Sheridan, Davie Morgan, George Smith, Jimmy Martin, Jessie Cresswell, Steve Harvey, Tommy Jopling. Front row: Billy Boyes, Ken Drysdale, Arthur Milligan, Eddie Crute, Brian Heskett and Mick McBay. Mascot: Thomas Mooney. Inset is manager Tucker Mooney who was in hospital on the day of the final.

North Star player Geordie Smith challenges BRSA (British Railways) goalkeeper during the final at Ryhope. North Star won the game 3-2 to lift the trophy for the 4th year in succession.

Grangetown Instrip, winners of the old Division 1 of the Sunderland Sunday League, Sunday League Knock-out Shield and the Bert Davies Memorial Trophy, 1980-81. Back row, left to right: S. Hunter, D. Hunter, J. Dickman, D. Stewart, D. Crosby, G. Fromme, G. Mills, D. Preece, H. Johnson. Front row: I. Laws, R. Crosby, T. Timm, G. Davies, J. Laws, R. Callaghan and W. Mitchell.

The strong Sunderland West End side which dominated the Wearside Combination League in the late 1940s and early '50s. West End won the league four seasons running from 1949 to 1952. Back row, left to right: John Barkess, Cyril Pape, Ken Goldsmith, Danny Rafferty, Richy Donkin, Mark Daily, Norman Hepple, Jack Reavaly, Bobby Coxon. Front row: Herbie Brown, John Donkin, Tommy Donkin, George Donkin and Kenny Johnson.

Grindon WMC, Wearside Combination League Second Division champions and winners of the J.S. Pears Memorial Trophy in 1983. Grindon snatched the trophy from Carley Hill YC after extra time by four goals to three. Back row, left to right: Norman Worthy, Dave Wood (captain), Eric Thomas, Barry Christie, Billy Wright, Steve Herron, Dave Bruce, Bob Young (trainer), Alan Loraine (manager), Harry Phillips. Front row: Harry Bradley, Don Richardson, Bob Pinder, John Rowntree, Kev Thompson, Kev Mason, Joe Dow, Ken Cleminson, Ron Ure and Ian Rackstaw.

The officials for the Grindon WMC versus Carley Hill YC final tie for the J.S. Pears Trophy are left to right: Billy Angus (linesman), the late Eddie Brannigan (referee) and the late Ray Foster (linesman). All three officials were well-respected referees on Wearside.

Intense Rivalry

Davie Conlon recalls: 'I can remember well the final of the Ken Atkinson Memorial Trophy at Belford House in 1983 between the Shelter Deck (now The North Star) and Southwick Social Club. Only a few yards separate the club and pub and the rivalry between the Southwick teams was intense. The two league games in the Sunderland & District League both ended in draws and the final was a fitting decider. The game wasn't AC Milan versus Inter but it felt like that to me. At half time it was 1-0 to the club but we had been kicking up-hill. In the second half and with the bank we won a penalty. I have played in many big local games but I've never felt so much pressure in taking that penalty. I was confident we would win if I converted it. It was a relief to score and owing to the tremendous passion and determination from every player on our side we overcame the club. And after I scored a second goal from outside of the box I can remember turning round in an arc to celebrate. As I was running past the opposing supporters with my fist in the air

Shelter Deck players celebrate the Ken Atkinson Memorial Trophy victory at the presentation night in the Shelter Deck pub

one of the women shouted some abuse at me. I was so elated it didn't bother me. Paddy McTiernan added a third which settled it. After we took the trophy back to the Shelter' some of the younger players decided to take it into Southwick Club and the rest of us followed. They were all sitting glum-faced. I suppose we shouldn't have gloated but the victory was so sweet.'

Peter Gibson, captain of the Shelter Deck after being presented with the Ken Atkinson Memorial Trophy on behalf of the team during the summer of 1983. Peter remembers: 'Beating our rivals, Southwick Club from across the road, was something special but the victory meant a little more to me because I played for Kenny Atkinson's Albion Sports Club from 1969 to 1971.'
Above right: Kenny Atkinson.

Presentation night for Hylton Lodge FC at the end of the 1977-78 season in Castletown Workmen's Club. The Sunderland & District League side were runners-up in the Ken Atkinson Memorial Trophy and the Wearmouth & Hylton Aged Miners' Cup. Professional footballer and Castletown lad Norman Bell, pictured front row, third from right, presented the trophies which included the Player of the Year trophy to his brother Alf (centre of front row). Norman Bell scored 17 goals in 80 League appearances for Wolves between 1975 and 1981. He transferred to Blackburn Rovers and from November 1981 to 1983 he scored 10 goals in 61 League appearances.

Michael Robinson, the Thorney Close WMC centre forward, receives his trophies from Brian Clough at the Sunderland & District League presentation evening in 1963.

Timpsonians

by Joe Cliff

Timpsonians in 1964. Back row, left to right: Herbie Hobson (trainer), Mickey Reeves, Jimmy Purvis, Peter Noble, Derek Phillips, Ritchie Allan, Jimmy Beverley (manager), Kenny Redman. Front row: Tucker Robson, Tucker Killala, Geordie Foster and Joe Cliff. Regulars missing from the photograph are: Jola Canavan, Ralphy Stubbs, Alan Harding, Brian Garret, Gordon Wainwright, Kenny Ellis and Dougie Crosby.

Timpsonians were founded around 1961. The name evolved from Sunderland Deaf which was a team of deaf people with speaking difficulties who worked for Timpsons shoe shops as shoe repairers/cobblers. Mickey Reeves was one of the first lads from the East End to play for them, but he didn't fancy telling anyone that he played for Sunderland Deaf so he used to say he played for Timpsons, then it became Timpsonians as they progressed. Timpsonians played in the Wearside Combination League and there were many successes over a six-year period including league, league cup and the Wearmouth Aged Miners' Cup. Some epic battles were had with teams from West End, Maplewood Star, Southwick Conservative Club and George Street Club. Many people agreed that Timpsonians were one of the finest footballing teams of that era. Some of the lads went on to play professionally, notably Peter Noble (Newcastle, Swindon and Burnley), Brian Garret (Cambridge), the late Kenny Ellis (Darlington) and Alan Harding (Lincoln and Darlington).

When the team first got a set of new strips in 1961-62, with the round crew neck which were orange in colour and with a set of blue ones for spare, they looked very fashionable. It was not unusual to see eight or nine of the team out together around the East End pubs and wearing the strips inside out or back to front to hide grass marks. I bet a lot of them still had their shorts on as well if the truth was known. I can never remember the team having any disagreements or arguments over anything. They really did play together, go out together and get on together. Timpsonians had a fanatical following from the East End of Sunderland but some of them got up to some tricks. During one game along Commercial Road they tied the opposition goalkeeper to the post for a laugh. And on another occasion the grass had been cut at the beginning of the season. It was dry like hay and some of the supporters set it alight and we had to play the game through a smoke screen. In about 1969 Timpsonians changed their name to Sunderland East End.

Right: A cartoon from the *Football Echo*, 6th December1952, of Wearside Combination League side Sunderland Deaf and Dumb Institute SC.

Below: Wearside Combination League side Sunderland Deaf and Dumb Institute SC in 1959. Back row, left to right: Alan Watson, Tony Armstrong, Brian Taylor, Donald Johnson, Alan Thornley, John Thornley, Eric Quinn, Tony Burn. Front row: ? Wilson, Jimmy Beverley, Raymond Fawcus, Leslie Reah, Brian Gunn and Fred Hardy.

Sunday League President's Cup Final
Cheers 0 Humbledon Plains Farm USL 4

Silksworth Park, 12th May 2002

Cheers' Shaun Godfrey (No 6) watches the outcome of his far post corner.

Plains Farm 'keeper Frankie Johnson clears his lines as Ian Wardropper attempts to close him down.

Wayne Mullen – Cheers' strong left sided midfield player.

Dean Arkley wins a midfield heading dual for Cheers.

Midfielder Dean Arkley takes on the Plains Farm defence. Looking on (right) is Plains Farm central defender Paul Robertson who had an outstanding game. Cheers' coach Tommy Dobbing said after the match: 'Although we are Premier League Champions Plainsy have been unbeaten in the Sunday League for four years and we went into the game as underdogs. We didn't perform well on the day and we didn't take our chances. I think that we are capable of beating Plainsy but I don't want to take anything away from them. They are a very good team and they deserved their victory.'

Cheers players applaud Humbledon Plains Farm captain Glenn Moan as he is presented with the President's Cup.

Glenn Moan with the President's Cup and his winners medal.

The Rise of Red House Club

Red House Workmen's Club's meteoric rise from the bottom of the Sunderland CIU League to the best Sunday league team in County Durham occurred when Billy Gray became manager.

Billy Gray remembers: 'We were the most consistent team in the Sunderland CIU League in the 1990s. Nobody could touch us. We won the league on seven occasions and the league cup three times. In 1992 we won the Durham FA Sunday Cup for the first time and repeated the success in 1993. At the end of the 1997-98 season the CIU League folded and Red House WMC joined the Wearside League's Second Division. We were champions at the first attempt in 1999 and we also lifted the prestigious Monkwearmouth Charity Cup. The following season we reached a respectable 5th position in the First Division. But it was costing us too much money to travel to some games and we were often under strength for some mid-week away games owing to some of the players not being able to get time off work to travel. We resigned from the Wearside League and joined the Sunderland Sunday League for the 2000-01 season. I look back with pride at what we have achieved over the past decade. We have developed from a struggling team which was in danger of folding and these years have been the best of my footballing life and I'll never forget them. The team of the early '90s which won the Durham Sunday Cup two seasons running had everything. I used local talent and I had 15 winners in my squad. They were exceptionally determined players who wanted to win every game. However, there are other factors which have brought about the success. Red House Club has backed and supported us; the committee have raised the finance for us; we have tremendous supporters that are second to none; and Trevor Henderson deserves a special mention because of his help to me as assistant manager.'

TABLES

SUNDERLAND SUNDAY LEAGUE
DIVISION I

	P	W	D	L	Pt
Plessey SC	20	15	1	4	31
Grangetown	18	13	3	2	29
Vaux Welfare	18	9	6	3	24
Cherry Knowles SC	19	9	4	6	22
Moore Paragon SC	19	7	6	6	20
Chesters	14	6	4	4	16
Torrens	16	6	3	7	15
Boldon Black Horse	20	5	4	11	14
Hastings Hill SC	17	5	3	9	13
*Grange Silverscreen	18	3	3	12	7
Downhill SC	19	2	1	16	5

*Two points deducted

DIVISION II

	P	W	D	L	Pt
Cleadon Britannia	19	15	2	2	32
Hylton Castle Club	18	11	3	4	25
Keith Oxman	20	11	3	6	25
T&W Fire Brig.	19	11	2	6	24
Vibroplant	16	10	3	3	23
North Star	20	8	3	9	19
Roker Victory Club	19	8	1	10	17
Burnside United	20	6	1	13	13
Seaham United	19	5	2	12	12
Bankhead Wanderers	19	3	3	13	9
Sunderland Companions	19	4	1	14	9

DIVISION III

	P	W	D	L	Pt
Boldon Grey Horse	20	17	2	1	33
Prospect United	20	13	5	2	31
Barnes Hotel	18	13	4	1	30
Sunderland P.T.E.	20	11	3	6	25
Houghton Lane	20	10	4	6	24
*Dubmire British Legion	20	8	4	8	18
†Ed. Thompson's SC	19	9	2	8	14
Ryhope WMC	19	4	3	12	11
Sunderland United	20	4	2	14	10
Homeworthy SC	20	2	1	17	5
‡Mountain Daisy	20	1	2	17	0

*Two points deducted
‡Four points deducted
†Six points deducted

DIVISION IV

	P	W	D	L	Pt
*Wear Gas S & SC	21	15	2	4	30
Thorney Close United	21	14	1	6	29
Selcray	18	13	2	3	28
Thistle	16	13	1	2	27
Sporting Club Victoria	22	10	5	7	25
Coles Cranes SC	22	9	4	9	22
Dunwoodie's SC	20	11	0	9	22
Seaham Comrades	21	9	4	8	22
Bummoor CFC	18	8	3	7	19
Ship Isis	20	5	2	13	12
S/land Water Co.	21	1	0	20	2
Whitburn Rangers	22	1	0	21	2

*Two points deducted

DIVISION V

	P	W	D	L	Pt
Penshaw Prospect	21	20	1	0	41
Roker Red Lion	22	18	2	2	38
Seaham Navy Club	23	15	3	5	33
F.H. Brickworks	23	15	1	7	31
S/land PWD Tech	24	10	5	9	25
Greens SC	25	9	5	11	23
Wearsider	24	8	6	10	22
Toll Bar	24	7	7	10	21
Savacentre SC	21	8	3	10	19
Cambridge Hotel	23	8	2	13	18
Earl Percy Rangers	25	7	3	15	17
Seaton Lane Inn	26	5	6	15	16
Washington B.L.	23	4	5	14	13
National Rovers	24	5	1	18	11

SUNDERLAND SUNDAY AFTERNOON LEAGUE
DIVISION I

	P	W	D	L	Pt
Dun Cow	15	11	3	1	25
Oaks	13	10	1	2	21
*Silksworth Wanderers	13	9	2	2	18
C.K. United	13	6	1	6	13
Garbutts TV	15	5	1	9	11
*Zhivago	14	6	1	7	11
Fulwell	12	4	1	7	9
Camrex	13	4	0	9	8
Sunderland County	16	1	2	13	4

*Two points deducted

DIVISION II

	P	W	D	L	Pt
Roker Derby	14	9	2	3	20
Boldon Cricket Club	13	7	3	3	17
Littlewoods	12	8	1	3	17
Albion Athletic	13	6	3	4	15
Blue Bell United	12	6	3	3	15
*Linskills	13	5	2	6	10
Sunderland Nomads	12	5	0	7	10
*Sporting Club Barnes	15	3	3	9	7
Cowies	16	2	1	13	5

*Two points deducted

SUNDERLAND C.I.U. SUNDAY LEAGUE

	P	W	D	L	Pt
H/don & Plains Farm	22	17	3	2	37
Murton Victoria	19	17	2	0	36
Seaham Labour Club	24	14	6	4	34
South Hylton	22	16	2	4	34
Silksworth Comrades	25	13	4	8	30
*Phili & H/ton	20	12	2	6	24
Washington SC	26	9	6	11	24
*Castletown	22	9	5	8	21
Farringdon	23	9	2	12	20
Silksworth RAOB	28	9	2	17	20
Town End Farm	23	9	2	12	20
Boldon SC	25	7	2	16	16
*Silksworth WMC	21	5	5	11	13
*Houghton Buffs	22	5	3	14	11
Red House	26	0	0	26	0

*Two points deducted

Sunday League tables, 5th May 1979. Note wooden spoonists Red House WMC – played 26 lost 26.

Red House Workmen's Club pictured after the replayed Durham FA Sunday Cup final in 1992 when Red House beat Jasprint Biddick Inn 1-0 at Ryhope. Standing, left to right: Billy Gray (manager), Tommy Henderson, Robbie Robinson, Frankie Spurs, Ian Lay, Alan Langley, Trevor Henderson, John Fannen, John Dow, Berwick Hall, Anthony Howarth, John Wake (secretary). Front row: Gary Fenwick, Freddie Patterson, Billie Lillie, Graham Boyes, Ian Nelson, Tony Nesbit and Freddie Gray. Mascot is Gavin Spurs.

What Football Teaches Us

In the early 1900s the Methodist Brotherhoods throughout the country identified the opportunity to tap in to the new spectator sport of association football as a source to attract men to the brotherhoods. In large towns and cities the brotherhoods organised 'Football Sundays' which were large organised gatherings of men who listened to guest speakers drawn from prominent players and officials from the Football League. The first Football Sunday in Sunderland took place in 1909 and it was such a success that another meeting, once again for men only, was organised on Sunday afternoon, 27th March 1910.

The Men's Homely Hour from the Ewesley Road Methodist Church created great interest in the town when they advertised that the principle speakers would be Dr Leigh R. Roose, Sunderland's famous goalkeeper or custodian as the 'keeper was known in those days, and Arthur Bridgett, Sunderland's England international left winger. Two thousand five hundred men, the majority of whom did not regularly attend brotherhood meetings, assembled in the Victoria Hall to listen to the talks. Unfortunately, Dr L.R. Roose was unable to attend because of another engagement but other Sunderland AFC footballers, as well as directors and officials of the club were present. Councillor Fred Taylor, chairman of Sunderland Football Club, and who had a Presbyterian background, presided and opened the meeting by praising the brotherhood movement for organising Football Sundays: 'Football Sundays,' he said, 'would not have been possible had it not been for the brotherhood movement. I do not think the church – and nobody respects the church more than I do – would have tackled it. I believe the churches do not tackle the masses, as they should do. The

Fred Taylor.

brotherhoods do and they are bringing the men over to the churches. The movement is getting hold of classes of men that the churches could never get at. Over one million persons watch football every Saturday and a large number of those do not attend any place of worship. It was for those that the brotherhoods existed. They have 600,000 members in the brotherhood movements who are to no small extent closely identified with football as players or spectators. It takes a very fine man to make a footballer, morally, spiritually and physically. He has to be a fit man otherwise he is no good for football and if for that reason alone I think the church should take an increased interest in the game.'

Arthur Bridgett.

When Arthur Bridgett, lay preacher and Sunderland's international winger with eleven caps, stood up to speak he received an enthusiastic reception from the audience. Arthur pointed out the importance of football in the development and moral training of young men. 'Football', he said, 'has been the means of cultivating friendships between men who would not otherwise have been brought together for the benefit of all concerned. Football has taught me the uselessness of selfishness, the silliness of conceit and the value of self-restraint. We live in times of strenuous activity when men need recreation to a certain extent and the finest recreation is to assist others in researching the Christ Jesus, a rock that never crumbles away. When men take a greater interest in their physical development they would take a greater interest in their spiritual welfare.' The meeting concluded and a collection was made which amounted to £17 18s 3d for the Brotherhood Sick and Benevolent Fund.

Despite the brotherhoods' promoting football they strongly opposed the game being played on a Sunday. The churches backed the FA's ban on Sunday football but teams like the Wellington Tavern (below) formed their own leagues and played on the Sabbath in spite of the national ban.

The Wellington Tavern, the unaffiliated Sunderland Sunday League champions, 1959. Back row, left to right: Sammy Cairns, Malcolm Scott, Ronnie Brown, Bobby Robson, Jimmy Christie, Walter Moss, Martin Gallagher, Terry Briggs holding his son Terry Jnr. Front row: Andy Carr, Bobby Burke, Rod Stokell, Norman Brown and Terry Burke.

SECTION FOUR

SOME OF THE LADS

A cartoon of St Patrick's Reserves from the *Football Echo*, 16th September 1950.

From Bishop's Boys' Club To Leeds United

by Arthur Rich

Bishop's were the leading under-18 team in the town and Football League scouts came to watch us. Fred Rodgerson and I were invited for trials to Leeds United and I signed professional forms for them. I was over the moon because it got me out of the shipyards, well, at least for a short while. I played centre half for Leeds United youth team when we won the Northern Intermediate

League in 1953. I progressed to the reserves but I made only one first team appearance. I was with Leeds until 1958 when I moved to Bradford Park Avenue in the old Fourth Division. After a season with them I returned home to work in the Sunderland shipyards and signed as a part-time professional for Spennymoor in the Midland League. Two or three seasons later Spennymoor joined the Northern League where it was amateur status only and pros were not allowed to play. I then moved on to Easington CW as a part-time pro for a short time. I was in my early thirties by this time and I finished my playing career with Pallion WMC in the Hetton CIU League, but I had to first apply for a permit from Durham FA to play as an amateur again. I played for Pallion until I was 37 when I decided to hang up my boots.

Arthur Rich during his Pallion playing days.

The successful Sunderland YOC Junior League side Bishop's Boys' Club pictured outside of Bishopwearmouth Church in about 1952. Back row, left to right: J. Ferry, T. Hazard, K. Noble, A. Rich, D. Gardiner, J. Sanderson, Mr Chapman (manager). Front row: K. Henry, J. Wilkinson, T. Taylor, K. Scorer, F. Rodgerson, N. Graham and Bobby Thompson (manager). Rich, Rodgerson and Taylor also played for Durham County Boys' Clubs XI. Two of the boys are wearing the Durham County Boys' Clubs' badge.

The team line-up taken from Manchester United's Reserves Programme for 27th October 1956. Right half Arthur Rich marked an inside left called Bobby Charlton. Arthur remembers: 'Charlton was only a 17 or 18-year-old and he was in and out of the first team at that time. I cannot remember much about the game other than they beat us 3-1. This fixture was of course before the Munich air

MANCHESTER UNITED RESERVES
RED SHIRTS AND WHITE KNICKERS

1
HAWKSWORTH

2   3
GREAVES   BENT

4   5   6
GOODWIN   BLANCHFLOWER   McGUINNESS

7   8   9   10   11
WEBSTER   DOHERTY   DAWSON   CHARLTON   SCANLON

Referee:
A. SMITH,
(Stoke-on-Trent.)

Linesmen:
A ARROWSMITH, (Red Flag.)
C CLAYTON, (Yellow Flag.)

11   10   9   8   7
TARRANT   FLYNN   McKENNA   JONES, David   WOODHOUSE

6   5   4
JONES, Dilwyn   HALLETT   RICH

3   2
ASHALL   LAWTON

1
NIMMO

LEEDS UNITED RESERVES
BLUE SHIRTS AND WHITE KNICKERS

disaster and some of the players who lined up against me were on the plane. Left back Geoff Bent was one of those who were killed. Left half Wilf McGuinness went on to play for England and became manager of Manchester United.'

Four Leeds United players in 1955. Left to right: Archie Gibson, Arthur Rich, Jackie Charlton and the great Welshman John Charles. The novelty of the photograph is that the four players are wearing plasters covering their split eyes and stitches. Arthur Rich remembers being understudy to John Charles and Jackie Charlton. John Charles moved from centre half to centre forward when Jackie Charlton came into the first team. Charles later played for Juventus and Arthur recalls him being the best in the world at both centre half and centre forward.

Geoff Hounslow – Football Fanatic

Geoff Hounslow (*right*) played in the local leagues for many years. His clubs included the Torrens, Ryhope Poplars, Roker Victory Club and The Dagmar in the over-40s league. A hard player and extremely fit, Geoff was diagnosed with a terminal illness in July 2000 and his last wish was to have his ashes sprinkled on Thompson Park football pitches. Geoff died in April 2001 aged 53 and his friends and former teammates organised a tribute game as a mark of respect to Geoff and to celebrate his contribution to the local football scene.

Geoff Hounslow's widow Freda fulfills Geoff's last wish and sprinkles his ashes on Thompson Park football pitches where he played so many games. The emotional ceremony was followed by a game in Geoff's memory between two of his former clubs – The Dagmar over-40s and Roker Victory Club. Left to right: Colin Davison, Dave Polly, Steve Hounslow (Geoff's son), Alan Hounslow (Geoff's brother) and Barry Davison.

The Dagmar over-40s and Roker Victory Club line up with Freda Hounslow before the tribute game to Geoff at Thompson Park on Sunday 20th May 2001. The game ended in a 4-4 draw.

Alan Mustard, 1956-1996

Kenny Mustard recalls: 'My son Alan hadn't played football for several years and when he turned forty he decided to play for Wearmouth over-40s. On 16th September 1996 our Alan collapsed and died on the Carley Hill ground in a game against Penshaw. Two of his sons were watching the match. Our Alan was also a good cricketer. He was a fast bowler and a hard-hitting batsman. He played for Hylton Cricket Club for many years. Alan's heart was with the young players and he managed the club's under-13 team. The club now have a trophy called the Alan Mustard Shield which is awarded annually to Hylton CC's junior player who represents the club in the best way. I cannot thank the Penshaw Club, Kevin Chisholm and Tucker Mooney from Wearmouth, enough for their fund raising efforts to provide a trust fund for Alan's three boys – Alan, Kevin and Philip – to enable them to buy sports equipment and travelling expenses. Particularly for Philip who plays for Durham County Cricket Club and was in the 22 strong England under-19 squad.

Eddie Robinson.

Eddie Robinson

Eddie was the eldest brother of the Robinson family from Thorney Close. He was an inside left or left winger, who captained Silksworth Colliery Juniors and was an amateur with Middlesbrough and Burnley before signing professional forms with Charlton Athletic in October 1954. Eddie was at Charlton for five years until he transferred to Cambridge United in the Southern League. His skill and goalscoring prowess soon made him popular with the home supporters. Shortly afterwards he signed for rivals Cambridge City and a local sports writer described Eddie as 'a dangerous forward, beautifully equipped both physically and in ability as a footballer – is a devastating raider with a lethal left foot.' In 1960 a serious knee injury ended 26-year-old Eddie Robinson's professional football career.

Alan Mustard.

Tommy Bewick of the East End

As a 19-year-old Tom Bewick of the East End played for Hood Street Methodists which won the All-Britain Methodist Cup in 1960. The following season Tom signed for South Shields and established himself as a regular first team player. Many fine performances for the Mariners earned wing half Tom a month's trial with Barnsley in March 1962 afterwards Tom returned home to Sunderland.

However, early in 1963 Tom and his wife Veronica emigrated to Australia and on arrival there he signed for Brisbane side Grange Thistle in the Queensland State First Division. Shortly afterwards Tom was picked to play for Queensland in the Australian Inter-State Championship. Tom and his wife moved to Melbourne where his career took him to Hakoah in the Victorian State League which was a higher class of football. Hakoah was the Jewish community's club side and Tom recalls: 'The former Israeli international Gerry Chaldy played for Hakoah and we played in other Australian States. It was an interesting experience and I was able to see much of Australia at the club's expense.' The family returned home to Sunderland but in 1967 they moved to South Africa where Tom played for Johannesberg outfit Germiston Caledonian in the South African National Football League Division One. Contemporary press reports of Tom Bewick's playing days at South Shields and abroad describe him as a strong, hardworking, tough defender who was extremely fit. He was County Durham Boys' Club Amateur Boxing Champion at welterweight in 1957 when he was 17. Tom put everything into his training sessions and he kept up his boxing interest with regular workouts in the gym. He eventually returned to Sunderland in 1974 and he played for local teams. For the past 21 years Tom has played in the Sunderland & District Over-40s League and he turned out for Marsden Inn for the 2001-02 season at the age of 62.

Tom Bewick (left) in action for Queensland State side Grange Thistle in 1963.

Tommy Dobbing – Player, Coach and Manager

Tommy Dobbing, a creative central midfield player and accurate passer of the ball in his playing days for Thorney Close Youth Club FC, the All-England Under-21 Champions of 1973. Tommy had represented Sunderland Juniors (under-11s) in the 1962-63 season. He was in the Southmoor School team that was Town and also County champions in 1967 and he played for Sunderland Boys under-16s in 1967-68. During the same season Tommy's natural leadership qualities were evident when he captained Lambton Street Boys' Club to a clean sweep in the YOC Minor League and they were also Durham County champions. To cap off a splendid season Tommy was selected to play for Durham County Boys. But it was while playing for East End SC in the Sunderland & District League in the 1971-72 season that 19-year-old Tom gained valuable experience playing in the same side with older men from his native East End. Tom recalls: 'It was a privilege being in the same team as some of the players that I watched when I was a schoolboy. They included Derek Phillips, Kenny Ellis, Mickey Reeves and Tommy Conroy. I definitely learnt my trade while playing with these men and they influenced me greatly.' Following the

Tommy Dobbing.

highly successful season with Thorney Close Youth Club which dominated the Sunderland & District League during the 1972-73 season, Tommy moved in to the Wearside League where he played for ten seasons with Silksworth, Ryhope and Easington. Later he played for Pennywell in the Washington Savacentre League and, after breaking an ankle at the age of 34, Tommy took up his FA Coaching Badge and became manager of Rolls Royce FC. Today 50-year-old Tommy is still as enthusiastic as ever about the game and during the 2001-02 season his well developed competitive and motivational qualities were utilized from the line as manager of Belford House and assistant manager/coach of Cheers in the Sunderland Sunday League.

Lambton Street, 1967-68, YOC Minor League treble winners and Durham County Cup winners. Back row, left to right: Peter Nichol, John Hawkins, Davie Hodgeson, Kenny Hiles, Jimmy Roffe, Derek Hunter. Front row: Richy Hughes, John McIntosh, Tommy Dobbing (captain), Davie Preece and Billy Palfreyman. Players missing from the photograph are: Dave Hadden, Mick Waller, Jimmy Harding and Mick Grant.

A Portuguese Adventure
by Tommy Clark

People were telling me that I was a good footballer and I thought I was good enough to play in the Football League. I was in my early twenties in the mid 1960s and I had played for Spennymoor and Bishop Auckland in the Northern League. In a game for Spennymoor against Sunderland Reserves at Roker Park in 1966 I was up against the likes of Colin Todd, Bobby Kerr and John O'Hare before they progressed to the first eleven. Nicky Sharkey and former England international Mike Hellawell were also playing. I knew that I had done very well against them and I was convinced I was good enough to play in a higher class. In 1965 I had played for Hitchin Town in the Isthmian League. We played West Ham United, the European Cup Winners' Cup holders, in a pre-season friendly. I thought West Ham's players were nowt special. In fact, even though I say so myself, I thought I was a better player than any of them. The press reported that I had an outstanding game and I was sure a club would come in for me, but nothing happened. By the late 1960s I was 27 and I was beginning to think that a professional career would pass me by, so I hitchhiked to Portugal to try my luck there. Being on the road was nothing to me. I had plenty of experience hitchhiking in this country and in Europe to work at holiday camps and fruit farms. I arrived in Coimbra (pronounced Queenbra), which is a large and beautiful student city, and I approached the local club who were in the Portuguese Third Division. Through an interpreter, because I couldn't speak a word of Portuguese, I told them that I thought I was a good player. I liked playing on dry grounds as I was a one-touch player and I told them that I wanted to play for them. Coimbra gave me a trial and then I signed professional forms for them. I had a great season with Coimbra and the highlight was the last game when we needed to beat Mira to win the league. On the morning of the game I can remember seeing large numbers of coaches full of our supporters passing our hotel. Coimbra must have emptied for the game. I had a lump in my throat. Our supporters were so passionate. They

Coimbra, wearing their Portuguese Third Division championship sashes in 1970. Tommy Clark is in the front row third from the right.

were worth a goal start. We beat Mira 2-0 and our supporters invaded the pitch. They mobbed us and stripped us of everything for mementoes. Shirts, shorts, boots and stockings were pulled off and the eleven of us eventually entered the dressing room ecstatic, high as kites and wearing only our jock straps. It was a fabulous day. Tom returned home to Sunderland after one season with Coimbra.

Tommy Clark curls in a centre for the incoming Coimbra forwards.

Tommy Clark in his playing days with Portuguese League side Coimbra.

Right: A cutting from a Southern newspaper report of the Hitchen Town v West Ham United friendly in 1965.

West Ham cracker

HITCHIN TOWN 3, WEST HAM UNITED 4
WHAT a thriller! Hitchin one goal up at half-time. Six goals in the second-half, including two spectacular headers from England's centre-forward, Johnny Byrne, and a third goal for Hitchin a minute from the end. There were 1,040 at Top Field on Tuesday for this excite-ment-packed game against First Division West Ham.

And as the last of the three centenary challenge matches opposition came to a close, it became more and more obvious that Hitchin had gained some valuable experience. An aggregate of 4-9 against three experienced professional clubs, including European Cup Winners' Cup-holders West Ham is certainly not discreditable.

After the match, team manager Cyril Buck said, "I feel Hitchin will do well this season now that the cloud has lifted; they are as good as any team in the Isthmian League."

BRILLIANT CLARK

All the Hitchin side fought bravely to the end. Outside-right, Tommy Clark played a sparkling game, and although the smallest man on the field he tackled courageously.

The first goal came when Terry CRADDOCK beat West Indian John W Charles with

John Wilkinson, Dusseldorf and the Northern League

John Wilkinson of Hendon began his National Service in 1954 as an 18-year-old. John had played for the successful Bishop's Boys' Club of 1952-53 season and he continued his football career with his regiment while stationed in Germany. Local Germans soon spotted John's skill, speed and goal scoring ability and Dusseldorf side Eller 04 signed him up. He is photographed below – front row, second from left. John recalls: 'I played centre forward for them and I scored a hat-trick in that game. Eller 04 was a big club. They had about 14 teams of various age groups and levels. I made some good mates in the junior team but older players in the club snubbed me. I think that it was because of the war. I made great friends with the goalkeeper who is next to me in the photograph. He would pick me up at the Army camp to play for Eller on Sunday mornings. I was the only English lad playing in the league and some of the opposing players liked to get stuck into the Englander. We won the league in my second season with them and I had some great times with the lads in bars after the game. They would pass around a large glass boot full of beer and the last one to take a drink had to pay to fill it up again, but they would never let me pay.

'After my National Service I signed for Bishop Auckland in 1957 and I scored about 50 goals for them in my three seasons at the club. In 1959-60 we won the Northern League Challenge Cup. I had the chance to turn professional with Huddersfield Town then managed by Bill Shankly but Bishops were looking after me. There wasn't much money in pro football in those days and I could earn more with my expenses and my job at Sunderland Docks. That was the reason why many leading amateur players wouldn't turn pro.

'After the Munich air disaster in February 1958 Bishop Auckland loaned Manchester United three of our players to help them out. As a big thank you United sent a team up to play Bishops in April 1959 but despite Bishops' 3-2 victory the game was disappointing. The *Northern Echo* reported: "The only thing that saved this game from being a complete flop was the performance of young Johnny Giles. But not far behind Giles was a great show put on by John Wilkinson, Bishops' outside right."

Eller 04 Juniors (under-20-year-olds). Champions of Dusseldorf, 1955-56.

'I had played my football mainly in the Northern League and I wasn't so well known in the minor leagues in Sunderland. In the late 1960s and early '70s I played for Ivy Leaf Club and Town End Farm Club in the Sunderland Sunday CIU League but I was getting on a bit and some defenders were kicking lumps out of me.

'Although I could look after myself on the field it wasn't worth risking losing work through injury so I decided to call it a day. I was proud that I went through the whole of my football career without being booked or sent off.'

Left: John Wilkinson in his playing days with Stanley United FC. John broke his leg in his first game for Stanley, which was in the FA Cup and, despite another broken leg later, John recovered to play for them from 1961 until 1973. He was in the side which won the Northern League Championship and Northern League Challenge Cup in 1961-62 season. John represented Durham FA for four seasons and won the FA Northern Counties Amateur Cup with them in 1962. He also played outside right for Northern Counties in an amateur international trial match against Southern Counties in October 1964.

Jack Washington and Wembley

Jack Washington (centre) lines up with his Bishop Auckland teammates before the FA Amateur Cup final in 1950. A crowd of over 80,000 witnessed Willington defeat their North East rivals and Northern League champions Bishop Auckland by four goals to nil. Jack played in two other FA Amateur Cup finals with Bishops. In 1939 a 20,000 crowd at Roker Park saw Bishops beat Willington 3-0, and in 1946 Bishops went down 2-3 to Barnet at Stamford Bridge in front of 60,000 spectators. Despite being a little more than 5ft 6ins tall Jack was recognised as a brilliant amateur goalkeeper, absolutely fearless and with remarkable agility and uncanny speed and anticipation. Jack was an athlete and a good all-round sportsman. In his prime he could run 100 yards in 10 seconds. A pupil at High Southwick Board School, Jack represented the town boys at both football and cricket; he played cricket for Sunderland first eleven for 30 years and represented the town at table tennis. Jack also played for St Columba's in the Church Institute League in the 1930s and after the war he became a physical education teacher at Hendon Board School.

Sadly, Jack passed away in August 2002 at the age of 88.

Tony Nesbit and England Schoolboys

Tony Nesbit of Red House Estate captained Sunderland Boys at under-11 and under-14 levels before he led Sunderland Boys under-15s to the English Schools Trophy win in 1983. Tony had signed schoolboy forms for Newcastle United when he was a 12-year-old pupil at Hylton Red House Comprehensive School. But despite the achievements of this talented and mature youngster the thrill of his selection to play for England Boys against Northern Ireland Boys at The Dell was undoubtedly the ultimate boyhood experience. Tony played in all of England Boys six games during the 1982-83 season which included two games at Wembley and the side were unbeaten winners of a six nations tournament. Tony became an apprentice footballer with Newcastle United when he left school in 1984 and he played in the Newcastle United side with Paul Gascoigne which won

Tony Nesbit with England shirt and cap.

the FA Youth Cup in 1985. Tony was a determined ball winner and a creative midfield player who prided himself in high workrate and one hundred per cent effort. He turned pro for Newcastle United in 1986 and he made his debut against Everton at Goodison Park in December of that year. Tony played for the first team six times before a serious knee injury eventually forced him to retire from the pro game in September 1987 at the age of 19. Tony returned briefly to the local football scene for Red House Workmen's Club in the Sunderland CIU Sunday League and he was in the side which won the Durham County Sunday Cup two seasons running – in 1991-92 and 1992-93.

Tony Nesbit in action for Sunderland Boys under-14s at Broadway School in March 1982.

Sunderland Boys under-14s in March 1982. Back row, left to right: Gary Mellefont, Ian Chandler, David Lilley, David Tate, Tony Knox, Chris Lindstedt, Mark McNally, Dale White. Front row: Stephen Smith, David Dodsworth, Tony Nesbit, Lindsley Pratt, Kevin Jopling and David Wilson. Five of the boys became professional footballers: Dale White (Sunderland), David Dodsworth (Leicester), Tony Nesbit (Newcastle), Kevin Jopling (Leicester and Grimsby), Ian Chandler (Barnsley). Ian scored the winner in Whitley Bay's FA Vase victory in 2002.

Right: Tony Nesbit (left) aged 15, with teammate Paul Gascoigne in 1983. The pair were playing for Newcastle United Youth team in the Aberdeen International Football Festival, which they won.

Billy Whittle of Hylton Castle Estate

Sunderland Sunday League side Hylton Castle WMC FC at the beginning of the 1986-87 season. Billy Whittle (20) is standing in the back row at the extreme left. The photograph was taken shortly before a tragic accident which ended this promising young player's life. On 15th October 1986 Billy was walking his dog when an articulated lorry hit him in a contraflow system on the A19 near to his home on the Hylton Castle Estate. Billy died instantly and his dog Jade had to be destroyed at the scene. Young Billy was a powerful central defender with a big heart and he has been sorely missed.

Billy Whittle of Hylton Castle 1966-86.

Left: The floral tribute to young Billy from his football club.

Gordon Howe

Gordon Howe, left back for the highly successful Hylton Colliery Juniors and Durham County Youth player, signed for Sunderland AFC in 1947 aged 17. Gordon played for Sunderland Reserves in the North Eastern League for two seasons before joining the Army where he served for five and a half years. Gordon remembers that he played a lot of good football in the Army where he converted to a centre forward. After leaving the military, Gordon played for Bicester Town in the Oxfordshire Hellenic League in the 1956-57 season and he had trials with Oldham Athletic and York City. In 1957 Gordon Howe returned to his native Sunderland and set about forming the unaffiliated Sunderland Sunday League. Gordon also started off the Sunderland and District Over-40s League and the Sunderland Over-35s League.

Gordon Howe in his playing days with Bicester Town.

George Lee Smith

Geordie Smith played for Hartlepool United Youth team in 1966 when Brian Clough was manager. John McGovern was another young lad in Cloughie's youth side and while Geordie settled down to a career in the local leagues after Hartlepool, Clough first took McGovern to Derby where they won the League and then to Nottingham Forest where he captained the side to a host of honours including two European Cup wins in 1979 and 1980. For many seasons Geordie turned out for three games over the weekend for top local sides. Geordie Smith was a hard competitor and a winner. He loved the game and he was the type that hated losing – at even cards or tiddlywinks. George was also a skilful midfield player with scoring ability. He had plenty of confidence and the local leagues lost a character when Smithy finished playing.

Geordie Smith, captain of the North Star, is presented with the Wearside Combination League Knock-out Cup in 1980.

Caseys, Old Boots and Lethal Studs

Stan Robson remembers the equipment used to play the game in the 1940s and '50s: 'There wasn't much money about in those days and I never owned a pair of shin pads but some players did. I used to push comics and cardboard down my stockings because protection was needed for shin bones against the old leather boots with hard toes. Leather bars or leather studs were nailed into the bottom of the boots and the studs could be lethal when they wore down or broke off exposing nails. If you came off a dry ground with all of your studs

intact you were lucky. Nails could also push through the soles and I used to place cardboard in my boots for protection. We also played with a heavy leather ball called a casey. We rubbed dubbin in it to try to keep the water out on wet days but it still became very heavy. I played centre forward and sometimes when I put a header in it knocked me dizzy for a few seconds. Heading the lace could also be hazardous and occasionally cut eyes were the result. On dry grounds the lace could distort the shape of the ball and it would bobble about. Sawdust or sand was used to mark out pitches. But the enclosed colliery grounds were the best to play on. They had a good playing surface and were marked off with white lines. There was also the luxury of nets on the goals, but of course the money was there from the pits. You had to pay to get into those grounds.'

Considering the equipment used to play the game in the 1940s and '50s this photograph is evidence of an extraordinary game which took place on Bishop Auckland's Kingsway ground when Bishops entertained a Nigerian FA eleven on 3rd September 1949. Nine of the Nigerians played with bandaged bare feet and the other two players wore only light shoes. Sunderland man Frankie Palmer takes on the visitors full back in front of 13,000 spectators. Bishops won the game 5-2. In 1949-50 Bishop Auckland were Northern League champions and they were runners-up in the FA Amateur Cup.

Since those naive barefoot days at Bishop Auckland in 1949 Nigeria have grown into a strong and talented footballing nation. They were Olympic Champions in 1996 and reached the finals of the World Cup in 2002. *Above*: Thorney Close lad Steve Howey challenges a Nigerian forward during his first game for England at Wembley in November 1994. England won the match 1-0.

Usworth football pitches off Ferryboat Lane on the outskirts of Hylton Castle Estate were used by generations of footballers before the Nissan car plant took over the site. But there weren't any changing rooms and Southwick FC are pictured getting stripped in Larry McGuinness' mobile shop in the late 1950s.

Sammy Hall and Lenny Chisholm

Sammy Hall (*right*), real name Fred, a well-built hard competitor and midfield ball winner. Sammy was also a good reader of the game and in the late 1960s and early '70s he played for Natcobos which came to dominate the Houghton & District League. Natcobos was a National Coal Board side based at Philadelphia Cricket Club and their home ground was Herrington CW. Occasionally Natcobos called upon Sammy to use his strength and pace as centre forward and in a league fixture with championship rivals Wingate Wanderers in March 1973 Sammy scored seven times in a 9-0 win. During this period Sammy played for Pennywell Comrades who were the top team in the Sunderland Sunday CIU League. He also had a spell with Wearside League side Whitburn. In the late 1970s Sam was part of the successful Torrens FC, winners of the Sunderland Sunday League Division One in 1976-77, and he was an influential player in the leading Wearside Combination League side Southwick North Star. However, Sammy recalls an occasion long after he had finished playing as one of his best memories of the local football scene: 'In April 2000 a birthday party was held for Lenny Chisholm in Pallion Workmen's Club. Former players from all over the area turned up for Lenny who was well respected in football circles. It was more like a footballers' reunion than a birthday party and it was great to see so many old friends again. Lenny was the hardest hitter of the T ball (the old leather casey) that I've ever seen.'

Wearside Combination side Southwick Conservative Club in the early 1960s. Players named only. Back row, left to right: Tommy Swinburne, LENNY CHISHOLM, Harry Bent, Brian Britton, Bobby Hazard, John James. Front: Tommy Johnson, John Doran, Roy Mills, Alan Bosher and Fred Tones. The photograph was taken at Joplings ground, South Hylton, before a cup final with Timpsonians which the Conservative Club won 3-1.

Lenny Chisholm, a big powerfully built inside forward with devastating shooting ability, also played for Horden in the North Regional League, Easington CW in the Wearside League and Herrington CW. While playing for Herrington in November 1961 Len equalled the club record of goals scored in a game when he cracked in six of the best against Fence Houses YMCA.

Tommy 'Horace' Henderson and Goals Galore

A skilful and stylish front runner with outstanding goalscoring ability, Tommy made a name for himself with Greenwell's in the Northern Alliance League in the early 1970s. Greenwell's manager Norman Clark, the former Ballymena United and Sunderland AFC player, set up an opportunity for Tom in 1975 to play for Ballymena in the Irish League. Tom recalls: 'Ballymena flew me from Newcastle airport to Belfast. When I arrived there, airport guards were carrying machine guns and I was met by Ballymena manager Arthur Stuart. He could see that I was worried but reassured me by the presence of two rather large bodyguards who were assigned to look after me. My first game was away to Larne and it was daunting running out on to their pitch in front of a 14,000 crowd. I had been accustomed to a few dozen spectators at Doxfields for Greenwell's. It was an old fashioned ground and the spectators were very close to the pitch. I was playing outside left and

In the 1978-79 season Tommy scored 62 goals for Seaham Red Star. He made a total of 276 appearances for the club and scored 211 goals.

I could hear, quite clearly, racial abuse directed at me from individuals in the crowd. After my second game I was approached by a director and the manager, who offered me a part-time contract and the promise of a full-time job. The people I had met in Northern Ireland were very friendly towards me. They were great people and I knew that my family would be alright. But my wife was worried about moving to Northern Ireland because of the troubles. So that ended my career with Ballymena after two games.'

Seaham Red Star in the late 1970s. Back row, left to right: Alan Gregory, Larry Phillips (manager), Dave Peacock, *Trevor Henderson, *Dave Preece, Bobby Davison, unknown, unknown, *TOMMY HENDERSON, Keith Peacock (secretary), Des Johnson. Front row: *Colin Tate, Nigel Dickenson, *Alan Laws, *Ray Moon (captain), Ian Stamp and Colin Fotland. In 1979 Red Star won the Phillips National Six-a-Side Tournament and received £9,000 worth of floodlighting equipment. In 1980 they won the Durham Challenge Cup at Roker Park by beating Boldon CA one nil and Sunderland lad Norman Taylor scored the winner. Red Star then completed the double in 1981-82 when they won the Wearside League and the League Knock-out Cup.

* Indicates Sunderland men.

Aubrey Stonely and Sunderland West End

Stan Robson recalls: 'When I was a boy I used to watch Sunderland West End towards the end of the war. They were based in an air raid precaution hut which was to the side of their home ground on what we called the Gunnies Field. There were four pitches there and one of them was enclosed where cup finals were played but the railings were pulled down during the war. The Gunnies Field was situated near to where the roundabout is now at the junction of Westmoor Road and St Luke's Road. European Way now cuts through the site and factories have been built there. Some great local players turned out for West End and they were a pleasure to watch. Aubrey Stonely stands out in my memory. He had attended Havelock School and he was blessed with a big physique. He was a rugged old fashioned centre half. He was a leader who marshalled his defence by telling players what to do and by keeping his full backs and half backs in check.

Below: Sunderland West End Wardens football team during the Second World War. Back row, left to right: Tutty Hackett, Billy McCain, Phillip Bolt, Richie Donkin, Eli Burton, D. Jurdson, Aubrey Stonely, Benny Appleby, 'Doc' Todd. Front row: Billy Tunstall, Tommy Coxon, Mr Willis manager of the post office in Pallion Road, Sammy Gardiner, D. Millar (secretary), Benny Crewe and Charlie Briggs.

Aubrey Stonely.

Andy Fannen of St Hilda's RC School was captain of Sunderland Boys for the 1951-52 season. Andy captained the town lads to the semi-final of the English Schools' Shield where they played out a 2-2 draw at Roker Park against Ilford Boys. The replay at Ilford resulted in a 1-0 defeat for Sunderland

Boys but the Ilford goal was a highly controversial decision when it was said that the ball did not cross the line. The *Sunderland Echo* described the result as a 'travesty of justice'. However, the *Echo* also reported that skipper Andy Fannen had an outstanding game: 'Fannen was here, there and everywhere … Fannen played a real captain's part and showed international form throughout.'

Tony Humble of Carley Hill Estate, a prolific goal scoring centre forward, Tony is physically well equipped for a footballer.

Two of his former managers remember him well. Tony Gibbon recalls: 'Tony Humble was only a young lad when he played for Hepworth & Grandage in the Washington Savacentre League but I could see that he was one of those players who was a natural forward and of course goal scorer. Tony was an intelligent footballer and a stylish player.' Nicky Pemberton recalls: 'Hub was at his peak when he played for Howard's FC in the mid to late 1990s. Not only was he an outstanding goal scorer but he was a good footballer as well.'

The Tunstall Hills Experience

In 1933 Sunderland Corporation released plans for football pitches, which had obviously been dreamt up by a person or persons with the imagination that football could be played on the top of Tunstall Hill! However, since then the five pitches with their various slopes and cambers have been the home grounds for generations of clubs. The Tunstall Hills experience began with the steep climb to the changing rooms and past the farm where players ran the gauntlet of aggressive geese, hens and the harassment of a Billy goat. Despite the panoramic view of Sunderland, Tunstall Hills is an exposed area where it is windy even on calm days. There are memories of playing there in the middle of winter in bitter conditions, and after the game being unable to fasten shirt buttons and shoe laces with frozen fingers. The match ball disappearing down the hill has always been a problem and there is the story of the goalkeeper who was having a nightmare game and his team was taking a hammering. He went to retrieve the ball but by the time he returned he had been substituted. In his disgust he booted the ball back down the hill. Playing football at Tunstall Hills was a challenge and an experience but the bleak conditions must have broken a few hearts.

Tony Gibbon (left) and Jessie Cresswell, twin strike force for Sunderland Sunday League side Thistle FC, pictured at the beginning of the 1981-82 season. Tony Gibbon, known as 'Bender', scored around 200 goals for the Thistle during a six-year period from 1976 to 1982 as the team progressed from the 5th Division to the 1st Division. Tony built his game around fitness and hard work. He had a wholehearted approach to the game and he was a good team man. Tony and Jessie formed a great partnership and laid on many goals for each other. They had a great understanding and could read each other's game. Jessie was a strong lad and a popular player for the Thistle. He was skilful and he had a goal scoring capacity with a powerful left foot. The Thistle lost Tony

Gibbon when he took up Shotokan Karate at the age of 29. He became a teacher in the sport in 1985 and he is now a 4th Dan. Thistle FC player/secretary Kevin O'Connor chose the black and white stripes that Tony and Jessie are wearing. Some of the players never forgave him for that!

Norman Morris pictured for Sunderland Boys during the 1960-61 season. Norman was the Southmoor School centre forward and their leading goal scorer. He signed schoolboy forms for Sunderland AFC and joined the club on leaving school. Norman remembers: 'Jimmy Montgomery lived near to me in Lichfield Road, Southwick and one Friday night he came to our house with a note from George Crowe the secretary. It said that I had to turn up the next day at 9 am with my boots. I wasn't sure what it meant but Monty, who was in the reserves at the time, told me that both Clough and Sharkey were injured. I was the youth side centre forward and I was so excited at the prospect getting a chance to play for the first team that I couldn't sleep that night. But when I turned up at Roker Park to travel with the team George Crowe told me that one of them had recovered and that I should take the day off. I was gutted, I was so near.' Norman was released after the 1963-64 season and he signed for Spennymoor in the Northern League.

AROUND THE TOWN

Town End Farm WMC in 1963. Players include: Barney Simpson, Charlie Simpson, Billy Innes, Billy Jopling, Henry Nelson, Billy McMurrough, Dennis Fox and the late Jimmy Green (goalkeeper).

The TLF Institute

The Thompson's, Laing's and the Forge combine provided leisure facilities for their apprentices and workmen at an institute situated in Fulwell Road near to Roker Park. The sports complex consisted of two football pitches, indoor training facilities as well as 5-a-side, billiards, snooker and table tennis. Peter Edwards, a former player for TLF Juniors from 1958 to 1961 recalls: 'Fred Burridge the groundsman kept the two pitches in absolutely first class condition and everybody admired them. The first pitch was called 'the institute' and the playing surface was like a bowling green. The other pitch 'the railway' was situated near to the railway line. TLF Juniors kicked off at 1 pm and on Sunderland's match days good crowds watched us before going to Roker Park. In the 1960s Sunderland AFC was interested to buy the TLF as a training ground but it was sold off for private housing development.'

Action photograph from a game in about the 1950-51 season between Wearside Apprentice League sides Sunderland Forge and Lynn's at the TLF ground in Fulwell Road. Lynn's are in stripes and the players from left to right are Martin Monaghan, Colin Robinson (heading the ball) and Ronnie Young.

Hetton Junior League side TLF Juniors in 1959. Back row left, to right: Peter Edwards, Brian Garrick, Alan Bent, Tommy Lamb, Keith Wilkinson. Front row: Billy Adams, Jim Baker, Billy Horton, Alan Black, Tommy Southern and Ray White.

Some of the players of Southwick RAOB at the presentation night after the 1970-71 season. The Buffs won the Wearside Combination League 5-a-side Cup and the Division 2 Knock-out Cup.

Star United, formerly Red Star, 1972-73. Back row, left to right: Ralph Hales (manager), George Laybourne, Tucker Mooney, Steve Clinton, Billy Gilboy, Joe Dagg, Eric Downes, Dennis Trout, John Conlon, Jimmy Watson. Front row: John Gallagher, Davie Conlon, Joe Moon, Geordie Tansey, Davie Dickinson, Terry Warren and Billy Blenkiron. Mascots: Graham Conlon (left) and Paul Moon. The Wearside Combination League side's impressive record:

1970-71 – Div 2 winners, Blind Institute Cup winners (as Red Star).
1971-72 – Div 1 runners-up, Blind Institute Cup winners, KO Cup winners (as Red Star).
1972-73 – Div 1 winners, KO Cup runners-up (as Star United).

Hylton Castle Blue Star, Sunderland Sunday League Division 5 winners
1971-72 and Division 4 runners-up 1972-73. Players include: Geordie Dawson,
Tommy Ramsey, Chris Hall, Gordon Thoms, the late Billy Lorraine (front row,
extreme left), Frankie Wake and the late Peter Fannen (front row, fourth from
left). Top scorer in the Division 5 Championship side was Chris Hall (back row,
third from left) with 40 goals.

Sunderland Sunday CIU League side Town End Farm WMC, about 1970.

Sunderland Jewish FC

Keith Oxman remembers his playing days with Sunderland Jewish FC: 'My brother Peter and I played for Sunderland Jewish in the Sunday League in the early 1970s. Our home pitch was at Tunstall Hills. They were Orthodox Jews and very nice people but they took some stick from opposition players and supporters. They were racially abused and persecuted and the number of Jewish players gradually dropped out until there was only centre forward Trevor Cohen and his brother Eric the goalkeeper left. The brothers were gentlemen and even though the rest of the players were non-Jews the racial abuse continued. By 1973 there was no reason to call the team Sunderland Jewish. The name was changed to Keith Oxman Cars and I sponsored them. Trevor and Eric Cohen played for us throughout the 1970s. Trevor was a strong lad and a prolific goalscorer. He had been an Israeli international.'

	ROKER SAINTS F.C.	
	FIXTURE LIST 1969-70.	
	An Official S.A.F.C.S.A. Team.	
DATE	OPPOSITION	VENUE
7. 9.69	Cliff United	Whitburn
14. 9.69	National Provincial Bank	Usworth No.3.
21. 9.69	Sunderland United	Whitburn
28. 9.69	Torrens F.C.	Thompson Park No.2.
5.10.69	Barclays Bank	Whitburn
12.10.69	Sunderland United	Tunstall Hill No.1.
19.10.69	Sunderland Shields Cup Tie	
26.10.69	Durham County Sunday Cup Tie	
2.11.69	Hylton Castle Arms	Whitburn
9.11.69	Barclays Bank	Tunstall Hill No.4.
16.11.69	National Provincial Bank	Whitburn
23.11.69	Cliff United	Usworth No.7.
30.11.69	Torrens F.C.	Whitburn
7.12.69	Hylton Castle Arms	Usworth No.4.
14.12.69	Sunderland Jewish	Tunstall Hill No.3.
21.12.69	Sunderland Jewish	Whitburn
28.12.69	Bee Hives S.C.	Thorndale Road
4. 1.70	Sunderland Taxes	Whitburn
11. 1.70	Lumley Brick Works	Whitburn
18. 1.70		
25. 1.70	Victoria Gardens	Thompson Park No.1.
1. 2.70	Sunderland Taxes	Vane Tempest
8. 2.70		
15. 2.70	Bee Hives S.C.	Whitburn
22. 2.70	Victoria Gardens	Whitburn
1. 3.70	Lumley Brick Works	Burnside Ground
8. 3.70	Lumley Brick Works	Whitburn
Manager:-J. Wallace, 1 Nelson Street, Sunderland.		

Above: Sunderland Sunday League Division 4 side Roker Saints FC's fixture list for the 1969-70 season. Roker Saints were an official Sunderland AFC supporters team and played on Sundays so as not to clash with matches. Their opponents in the league included Sunderland Jewish who played on Sunday rather than Saturday which was their Sabbath. Hylton Castle Arms were Division Four champions in 1969-70 and the Torrens were runners-up. The Torrens were also runners-up to Downhill WMC in the League Knock-out Cup. The Torrens went from strength to strength in the following two seasons by winning the 3rd and 2nd divisions without dropping a point and they became the leading Sunday League side.

Keith Oxman Cars in about 1975. Back row, left to right: S. Thompson, P. McGinty, D. Pearson, unknown, P. Oxman, unknown, unknown. Front row: A. Warriner, E. Cohen, T. Cohen, M. Lovstad and A. King.

Fulwell CAYS, 1962-63, winners of the North East Durham Junior Cup,
Michael Oxberry Memorial Cup (left) and the Alder Charity Cup (right). Back
row, left to right: Mr R. Wilson, Mr G. Holt, D. Pillans, S. Robertson, G. Liddle,
D. Wilson, D. Craggs, J. Anderson, Reg Watson (manager). Front row: J. Little,
G. Marrs, R. Irving, R. Kennedy, R. Brown, G. Wainwright, G. Blyth and Mr J.
Grieves. Following this successful season Ronnie Brown was invited to Arsenal
for trials. He eventually signed for Blackpool.

Sunderland & District side Grindon WMC, Blind Institute Cup runners-up at
the Hospitals Ground, Newcastle Road, about 1978. Back row, left to right:
unknown, Mickey Taylor (manager), Kenny Hutchinson, Mid Royal, Les West,
Trevor Hutcheon, unknown, Keith Machin, Brian Sinclair, Davie Ferry, Trevor
Hutcheon's dad. Front row: Tommy Howe, Jack Johnson, Ralphy Taylor, Owen
Williamson, unknown, Ian Palfreyman and Bobby Pinder.

Aquatic Sports in January 1978. Back row, left to right: Karl Wandless, Edward Oliver, Joe Ashton, Tom Oliver, Phil Andrews, Kenny Jenner, David Wake. Front row: Stan Willey, Paul Duningham, Brian Callaghan, Mickey Smith and David Farrer, plus mascot.

Founder club member David Craggs remembers: 'We were a group of friends that used to drink in the Aquatic Arms which was a pub situated very near to Wearmouth Bridge. Next door was the Royal Hotel and in the side street was the Engineers and across North Bridge Street was the Oak Tree. We decided to form a football team and entered the Combination League for the 1962-63 season. Eddie and Tom Oliver were other founder members. We paid half-a-crown per week subs and we paid sixpence on top of that for every goal conceded. We took some hammerings but the kitty soon mounted up and the lads couldn't wait until the end of the season when we organised a good night out drinking, night-clubbing and we had more than enough money in the kitty to hire a bus for transport. Tommy Oliver is still with the club today as secretary.'

North Bridge Street in 1970. The Aquatic pub is adjoining the Royal Hotel.

The Origins of Sporting Club Vaux FC

by Trevor Whitehead

On Friday, 8th May 1987 at the Vaux Sports ground in Glenesk Road, Sunderland, SC Vaux from the Wearside League won the prestigious Shipowners' Cup by beating Murton CW 2-1 in a replay, after being held to a 1-1 draw in the first game at Murton Colliery Welfare. On paper, and to the uninitiated, this may appear to be something of a non-event, something which is repeated at sports grounds all over the country. But to the players, managers, committeemen and supporters of the club it was a historic achievement and something, which was little more than a pipe dream some twenty years earlier.

In 1966, Brian Hill created a team called Monkwearmouth College of Ex Students and entered the team into the Saturday morning Tees-Wear College League. The following season they resigned from this league and entered the Tyne-Wear Saturday morning league under the name of Bishopwearmouth FC.

In the 1968-69 season Brian Hill together with friends Alan Bosher and Bob Forster successfully applied to take Bishopwearmouth FC into the North Eastern Amateur League. It was there that they remained for a number of seasons winning both league and cups along the way. It was due to this success, however, that the club began to grow. Due to the number of players wishing to join the club and the limited number of opportunities allowing for one team it was eventually decided to expand the club and the call went out for extra players.

In the1975-76 season the Bishopwearmouth second team was formed under the guidance of George Hunter (secretary/manager) and they entered the Second Division of the North Eastern Amateur League. Both teams at this time were playing at the South Hetton Colliery Welfare Ground. A ground blessed with two excellent pitches, situated front and back of the pavilion/dressing

SC Vaux, Shipowners' Cup winners, 1986-87. Back row, left to right: Billy Cruddas (manager), unknown, Brian Jennings, Les Frizzell, Tom Callaghan, Davie Lawson, Steve Golightly, George Cook, John Lang, Keith Robertson, Dave Callaghan, Ray Banks. Front row: Alan Scott, Willie Moat, Tom Owens, Derek Holden, Dean Ferry, Steve Hertzeg and Tony Clark (assistant manager).

rooms. The two teams were successful in their respective leagues and there was a tremendous family type atmosphere with wives and children actively involved in the club.

The early 1980s was an exciting stage in the club's development. This progress was due to a large squad of young and extremely talented young men joining us en-masse from Grindon Boys' Club – Steve Binks, Gordon Rodenby, Joe Clark and Steve Purcell to name a few. The success at both levels continued but a growing unrest was felt within the club. It was determined that whilst the club's resources were excellent in the form of playing staff, committee members, money, pitch, dressing room facilities and equipment the standard of competition from the league did not match our ambitions.

In the 1983-84 season the club took a massive step in its development. In spite of the concerns of people in the world of amateur football in Sunderland, they applied for and were successful in their application for the first team to join the Wearside League. The second team, after winning the North Eastern Amateur League Second Division championship, applied for and gained promotion to the NEAL First Division. They were successful in their application for now, without the first team to bar their way, they were allowed entry to the First Division. The North Eastern Amateur League was at the time a 'gentleman's league' with true amateur league status. Players were not required to sign on and only one team from any club was allowed in any one division, hence the refusal by the league to allow the Bishopwearmouth second team entry to the First Division, although they had won the Second Division championship on numerous occasions.

On successful application to the Wearside League it was felt appropriate, although sadly, to drop the name of Bishopwearmouth and adopt the name of the village from where the club played – South Hetton, a small mining community in County Durham. We became known as South Hetton CWFC.

On Saturday 20th August 1983 the first match in the Wearside League was played at South Hetton Colliery Welfare, with South Hetton FC losing 1-2 to the more experienced South Shields FC. The team remained rooted to the bottom of the league all season but everyone associated with the club relished the far higher standard of football they had ever encountered. As the club committee carried out an analysis of the future of the first team, the second team went from strength to strength in their new found freedom in the First Division. The change and development did not, however, rest there. The analysis of the first team identified the need to compete at this higher level. Unfortunately the desire to succeed became dependent on finance and the ability to attract newer and better players to the club. An application was made to the Sunderland-based Vaux Brewery for sponsorship. This was achieved at a price. The sponsorship on offer was dependent on the club changing its name and relocating to the Vaux sports ground situated in a beautiful part of Sunderland with Tunstall Hills as its backdrop. The decision was made to accept the offer and sadly we left our roots at South Hetton and moved to Sunderland.

A slight problem was encountered in the beginning as there were already existing teams playing under the banner of Vaux (Saturday afternoon and Sunday morning), both of whom were already based at the Vaux sports ground. After very careful and delicate negotiations it was agreed to accommodate the existing teams into the fold of the club and offer them all of the facilities of the big club status. To accommodate the extra team a successful application was made to the Washington Savacentre League for the SC Vaux Reserve FC side. In the 1984-85 season the club was re-named Sporting Club Vaux FC. This was as the result of a request from the then Managing Director of Vaux, Mr Frank Nicholson, who wanted the name of Vaux to be synonymous with sporting excellence in Sunderland. To complete the circle it was decided by popular demand to secure the future of the club by adopting an existing youth team into the fold. Coles Cranes Juniors was a very successful youth team who played in the Hetton Youth League, under the masterful guidance of Mr Malcolm (Mac) Scott. They were taken under the wing of the Sporting Club Vaux banner with the intention of re-naming them SC Vaux Juniors. This idea was discounted by the then Durham FA secretary John Walsh, as an agreement was in place not to allow any team under the age of 18 to be associated with any linkage to alcohol or cigarettes. They were subsequently re-named SC Glenesk in honour of the address of the Vaux sports ground. They repaid their gratitude by winning the Durham County Youth Cup in the 1986-87 season. The commencement of the 1984-85 season saw the club boasting five teams within its ranks, these included: Sporting Club Vaux FC (Wearside League), Sporting Club Vaux Reserves FC (Washington Savacentre League), Bishopwearmouth FC (North Eastern Amateur League), Vaux United (Sunderland Sunday League) and SC Glenesk Juniors (Hetton Youth League).

And so on to 1986-87 and the Shipowners' Cup success. The finale to the story is a sad affair. In the late 1980s the financial decline of the Vaux brewery

Bishopwearmouth (front row) and Bishopwearmouth 'A' line up in the late 1970s. Back row, left to right: George Hunter (secretary/manager), Brian Lamb, Les Hewitt, Dave Griffith, John Bowmaker, Steve Donkin, John Taggart, Trevor Whitehead, Bob Langley, Dave Armstrong, Paul Gillespie, Kev Wardle, Alan Snowdon, Malcolm Johnson, Norman Griffin, Les Cain. Front row: Duncan Ramsay, John Goodchild, Cuth Earl, John Forster, Jim Fenwick, Dave Lane, Matty Edmundson, Alan Usher with son Ian, Trevor Robson, Alan Bosher, Brian Hill, George Smith and Bob Forster. It is interesting to point out that John Forster pictured in the front row, fourth from the left played full back for Ryhope CW when they met Workington Town in the 1st round proper of the FA Cup in December 1967. Ryhope were beaten 0-1 but nevertheless it was a remarkable achievement for a colliery welfare side.

began to materialise. The first move that affected the status of the club was the selling of its beautiful sports ground at Glenesk Road at the end of the 1987-88 season to make way for a private housing development.

At the end of the 1988-89 season the club were left with little alternative but to seek a partner to share their expenses. The original club was left with players, committee members, equipment and the expertise to run a successful club – but no ground.

During the close season prior to the commencement of the 1989-90 season, it came to the attention of the SC Vaux club that Ryhope CW was in danger of going out of existence unless an amalgamation with another club could be found. Ryhope CW from the Wearside League could boast little or none of the attributes of SC Vaux, but they had an existing and recognised Wearside League ground. Contact was made between the clubs and the subsequent merger took place. The story of the club therefore continued under the amalgamation of Sporting Club Vaux and Ryhope Colliery Welfare FC, and under the grand title of Vaux Ryhope Colliery Welfare FC.

Unfortunately, at the end of the 1990-91 season the sponsorship with Vaux came to an end and the title 'Vaux' was dropped from the name. The club reverted back to the name of Ryhope CWFC, as it still stands today. The old committee of SC Vaux, who had taken the club so far over a period of twenty years, retired gracefully and a new committee took over the reins. A club had been born and died in a matter of 20 years.

SC Vaux players who had experience with Football League clubs included: Nigel Saddington (Doncaster, Carlisle and Sunderland), Graham Bassett (Sunderland), Ronnie Robinson (Leeds United), George Cook (Burnley), Kenny Mitchell (Newcastle United), Mick Smith (Wimbledon), Tim Gilbert (Sunderland) and Tom and Dave Callaghan (Sunderland).

NORTH EASTERN AMATEUR LEAGUE

DIVISION I

	P	W	D	L	F	A	Pt
Bishopwearmouth	30	22	5	3	80	28	49
Belford House	30	19	6	5	80	39	44
Electrosil	30	21	2	7	73	43	44
Nothern Coun DB	30	17	8	5	71	31	42
Met. Fire Brig.	30	14	7	9	76	67	35
S'land Harlequins	30	12	7	11	69	68	31
Newcastle Poly	30	11	8	11	59	64	30
Hylton Castle	30	12	5	13	63	63	29
Coles Cranes	30	11	7	12	53	54	29
Durham Cavaliers	30	12	5	13	59	62	29
Reyrolle A	30	12	4	14	76	74	28
N'castle Un Emp	30	10	3	17	71	85	23
Bohemians A	30	7	5	18	48	94	19
Roker Harlequins	30	6	5	19	38	73	17
Telephone Alb	30	6	4	20	42	74	16
N'castle Un Res	30	5	5	20	35	72	15

DIVISION II

	P	W	D	L	F	A	Pt
Bishop'mouth A	34	24	5	5	115	43	53
KOSA	34	22	9	3	91	41	53
Vaux Utd	34	22	8	4	94	48	52
Cornings	34	21	6	7	101	52	48
BRSA	34	21	4	9	114	81	46
Sunderland Poly	34	17	8	9	88	78	42
*Hillheads Marl	34	17	6	11	81	53	38
Belford House A	34	13	9	12	66	57	35
S'land Harl A	34	15	5	14	81	79	35
David Brown	34	12	9	13	62	62	33
Met Fire Brig A	34	13	5	16	56	64	31
N'thern C'ts A	34	11	4	19	62	89	26
Old Bedans	33	10	4	19	76	111	24
Tel Albion A	34	10	3	21	55	91	23
Newcastle Univ A	34	6	7	21	48	99	19
Ryehill Sports	34	7	4	23	67	115	18
W'ton Acads A	34	4	8	22	47	88	16
Medicals	33	6	4	23	44	91	16

Final tables 1981-82 season.

The Coles Cranes Trophy final at Coles Cranes ground in 1983 when Bishopwearmouth 'A' beat Belford House 4-2 (after extra time). John Forster, in the white strip nearest the camera, scores the first goal for Bishop's after 15 minutes.

Bishopwearmouth 'A', pictured with the first team's North Eastern Amateur League's First Division Championship Trophy, the NEAL Shield and their Second Division Championship Cup in 1982. Back row, left to right: Trevor Whitehead (secretary/manager), Tony Edmundson, Mick Reay, Malcolm Dryden, Kevin Wardle, Mick Maddison, Nick Lumsdon, Alan Snowdon, Alan Bosher (manager). Front row: John Forster, Neil Hindhaugh, Gordon Snowdon, David Lane, Brian Mann, Johnny Whelam, Steve Robinson and mascot.

Representatives of SC Vaux's five teams in a committee meeting in the mid 1980s. The meeting was held in the Vaux Social Club in Green Street. The site is now occupied by St Mary's multi-storey car park.

The Sunderland & District Over-40s League

A jubilant Southwick Social Club, winners of the first ever Over-40s League Knock-out Cup in 1981. Gordon Howe, founder of the Sunderland & District Over-40s League, is in the back row extreme left in track suit top. Lenny Chisholm, pictured kneeling in front of Gordon, scored all three goals in the 3-0 victory over rivals Hepworth & Grandage.

The Sunderland & District Over-40s League was formed in 1980 by Gordon Howe. There were eight original clubs and in 1981 thirteen clubs entered the League when Gordon Howe is recorded as founder and president with Kip Watson as secretary and Derek Snaith as treasurer. The Over-40s League continued to grow and two divisions were created for the 1983-84 season to accommodate twenty clubs. Gordon Howe left the Over-40s League to set up the Sunderland Over-35s League in 1983 but the foundations had been laid and the success of the Over-40s League has been phenomenal. The Sunderland Catholic Club Over-40s League contained 63 clubs which competed in five divisions in the 2001-02 season.

This keen trio of over-40s braving the cold in January 1992 to train on Roker beach would probably put many younger players to shame. Left to right: Gordon Carty, Tony Braid and Ted Wooton.

Sunderland Sunday CIU League side Ivy Leaf Club in 1968.

Binns Sports Club, about 1950. Back row, left to right: Pearson, Murdy, Kitchin, Conroy, Howe, unknown, Collier, Mr Hartford (manager). Front row: Milburn (trainer), Dunn, unknown, Carr (captain), Todd and Webster. Doug Carr remembers: 'I played for Binns for about five seasons in the Wearside Combination League. Our home pitch was at Binns Sports Ground at Newcastle Road. It had an excellent playing surface and later Hospitals Sports Club took over the ground. The photograph brings back happy memories of a time when there were so many different teams and leagues. After Binns folded I played for Sunderland West End. They had many successful seasons and the Donkin family always represented them. We played at home at Ford Park and also at Joplings and Forsters enclosed ground at South Hylton.'

Sunderland Hospitals Sports and Social Club, about 1980. Back row, left to right: Jimmy Barrass, Mark Hewitson, John Smith, Kenny Payne, Stan Wood, Neil Smith, Ronnie Cooper, Alan Croft. Front: Harry Clark, Vic Broncz, Dave Payne, Dave Weston and Joe Sumner.

Hetton CIU League side the Transport Club, 1980-81. Back row, left to right: John Shergold (manager) with mascot – son Mark, John Burke, Mick Mersh, Chris Kirby, Ray Henderson, Joe Dagg, Peter Boyle, Kevin Thompson, Kevin Snowdon, Ernie Harrison, Derek Jones, Alan Dunn, Geordie Tansey. Front row: Tom Agnew, Ron Cowie, Tom Steabler, Eddie Crute, Davie Conlon, Nick Pemberton and Peter Charlton. Mascots, left to right: Gary Tansey, Ian Conlon, Maxine Conlon and Alan Dunn Jnr.

Sunderland East End Community Association, 1957-58. Back row, left to right: Ray Clancy, Billy Moore, Billy Brown, George Alder, Sid Swales (captain), Les Ward, John Moore, Ray Clancy, Tommy Sirmond, Tommy Mutch. Front row: Terry Waugh, Tommy Sawyer, Kit Henry, Les Ward, Terry Worthy and Ernie Dawson. The team, who competed in the Wearside Combination League, line up on their Town Moor pitch. Notice there is no net and the sawdust pitch markings. Kit Henry remembers that sawdust obtained from nearby Thompson's sawmill was used because the cinder-covered pitch would not take a white line. Kit said: 'One Saturday morning we marked out the pitch with sawdust but there was a heavy downpour which washed away the lines and we had to mark them out again just before the kick-off. It's funny looking back at that. The Town Moor was hard to play on. You had to be careful when tackling but even so the cinders caused scraped legs. We had more blue line scars than pitmen! We used to get some good crowds watching us at home games when the bars came out at 3 o'clock.' In the background is Burliegh Garth and in front of the Garth is Grey School. The building on the left behind the wall is Trafalgar Square.

The Stolen Goal

In 1969 East End played Town End Farm WMC at Thompson Park in what was the decider for the Wearside Combination League Division One title. A player involved in the game remembers an incident which prematurely ended the match: 'After the kick-off a gang of East End supporters appeared on the scene. They'd been on the drink and the atmosphere became intimidating. Two or three of them started swinging on the crossbar. In those days the goals were made of wood. There were no nets and the square posts fitted into slots in the ground. On the half-hour, Town End Farm broke away and scored and the East End supporters weren't happy about it. Some of them were talking about stopping the game. The next thing I knew they lifted the posts of one of the goals out of the ground and carried off the whole goal. If I can remember rightly they then smashed the crossbar. The referee asked somebody to go for a policeman but nobody would, so he abandoned the game. The rearranged match ended 3-0 to Town End Farm and they won the league.'

Sunderland & District League side Joplings in about 1970. Players only in strips named, Back row, from left to right: Tommy Steabler, Doug Weir, Peter Edwards, Joe Flett, Jimmy Gibson, Joe Dow, Jock Hatton. Front row: unknown, Ray Foster, Geordie Smith, Ray Allen and Bobby Lincoln.

Thorney Close FC, a successful Sunderland & District League side, in about 1969-70 season. Back row, left to right: Malcolm Johnson (manager), John Turnbull, Lenny Thornton, Bucky Thoms, David Appleton, Arthur Henderson, Alan King, Alec Johnson Snr. Front: John Young, Ken Maskell, Ashy Spooner, Bob Taylor, Ray Moon and Billy Thornton.

Ewesley Road Methodists FC at a function at Carlton House in 1950.

The Hastings Hill, early 1970s. Notice that three players are wearing headbands to hold back fashionable long hair.

Torrens FC, Sunderland Sunday League Division One champions, 1976-77. Back row, left to right: Tommy Henderson, Eric Simpson, Eddie Etherington, Alan Goldsmith (captain), Derek Jones, Sammy Hall, Pat Tansey, Alf Goldsmith (manager). Front row: Richie Wooler, Keith Wooler, George Smith, Bobby Lincoln and Stan Craig.

Wearside Combination League side Sunderland Deaf and Dumb Institute SC on Wearmouth Colliery Welfare ground in 1945. Back row, left to right: Wilson, Reah, Aitchison, Beverley, Johnson, Parkinson. Front: Cliff, McCletche, Parker, Collins and Hardy.

The Wolseley, Sunderland Sunday League Division 2 champions and League Knock-out Cup winners in the 1980s. Those pictured include: Jessie Cresswell, Denny Mole, Neil Heslop, Steve Murray, Brian Lamb, Kevin Harrop, Kevin Simpson, Arthur Watson, Don Richardson, Ian McGill and Tom Weldon.

Wearside Combination League side Clarks United, 1949-50. Back row, left to right (players only): J. Myers, T. Bowen, T. Murphy, E. Neill, A. Smith, S. Kayl. Front row: T. Leadbitter, R. Cockburn, R. Carty, G. Hall and A. Brown. Ron Carty was the League's top scorer in 1948-49 season with 74 goals.

A Canny Day Out

by Peter Gibson

I played for Southwick Social Club in the Hetton CIU League and it was a canny day out. After the game on a Saturday morning the home club provided a pint and a pie/sandwich as hospitality for the away team. Competitive darts and dominoes followed and side bets were placed (on the quiet). Sometimes a lot of money was resting on the first player to reach five chalks. It was interesting visiting the County Durham pit villages and their dialects varied from village to village. They used words like thou, thy, thee, the knarrs, marra and ow-lar. Whippet racing was popular with older men bearing blue line scars on their faces and arms after years of working underground. The Hetton CIU League provided the venue for some good, hard football matches and we were all up for it. We had to be prepared because their supporters gave us townies some stick which gave us the incentive to win those 50-50 balls.

Our team manager was Tommy Young, or TY as he was known to us, and he was a real character. He would leave the side-line at Marley Pots to collect the sandwiches and saveloys from a butchers shop at Pennywell for after the game. It was strange that the team manager should leave the game like that but TY had his priorities right.

Davie Conlon remembers: 'During a game at Marley Pots I was injured and I had to come off. TY said to me: "I've got just the thing for you Davie boy." TY opened up his top coat to reveal a row of saveloys lined up like cigars in his inside pocket. TY pulled one out and pushed it into my hand. "There you are son," he said as he patted me on the back and winked. I was in so much discomfort that eating a large saveloy was the last thing on my mind. But I said: "Thanks Tom."'

Hetton CIU League side Southwick Social Club FC, 1979-80. Standing from left to right: Dickie Conlon, Sammy Conlon, Sammy Hall, Mickey Pemberton, Geordie Dixon, Ernie Harrison, Kevin Harding, Tommy Tansey, Tommy Young (manager), Eddie Wooton, Michael Henderson (referee). Front row: Geordie Smith, Jonty Pemberton, Nicky Pemberton, Eddie Crute, Davie Conlon and Gordon Mason (Shack). Insets: Peter Gibson (left) and Kevin Snowdon.

Gordon Mason remembers: 'One Saturday morning we had played a club team in one of the pit villages and we went back to their club for the pie and pint in the lounge. But after that there followed a steady stream of food. We appreciated their hospitality and scranned the lot! Eventually a barmaid, holding another tray full of roast potatoes, popped her head around the door. "You's are the whippet men aren't you's?" She asked. "Not now we're not." said TY as he laughed and rubbed his full stomach, which was followed by loud laughter from the rest of us. There had been a whippet meeting in an upstairs room but they had mistakenly brought us the food. It was a scream.'

It was an experience playing for Southwick Club but it could be rough when the inevitable internal disagreements took place. There was a game when we won a free kick on the edge of the box. Both Sammy Hall and Davie Conlon stepped up to take it and neither would back down. The argument developed in to a scuffle which was broken up. 'I'll see you after the game,' was the usual threat and in TY's van Sammy and Davie kicked-off again. The rest of us were trying to stop it and the van was rocking from side to side with TY noncholently driving it down Old Mill Road without a care in the world while there was hell-on in the back of the van. They were eventually separated and when things had calmed down TY said: 'Well lads, it's the Boilermakers next week.' As though nothing had happened. He was a dry 'un was TY!

The caricatures of a Southwick team from another era. St Hilda's Sports Club, *Football Echo*, 7th October 1950.

Southwick Community Association Football Club, 1984-85. Back row, left to right: Len Christopher (manager), Ken Drysdale, Keith Baker, Glen Baker, Chris Riley, John Massingham, Ian Hartley, Mick Cockburn, Ed Christopher (assistant manager). Front row: Tim Skinner, Geoff Hay, Dave Gales, Bobby Cockburn, Dave Stobbart and Norman Purnell. Len Christopher recalls: 'I took over as secretary of Southwick CA with Malcolm Keenan (who was on Sunderland's books and later played for Cambridge City) as player manager. In 1981-82 we won the Sunderland & District League. We were elected to the Wearside Combination League Division 3 for the 1984-85 season and I became manager/secretary after Malcolm moved on to Wearmouth Colliery. In consecutive seasons we won the Div 3, Div 2 and Div 1 titles to win promotion to the Premier League. We also won the Jim Pears Trophy and were runners-up to Hepworth & Grandage in the Wearmouth & Hylton Aged Miners' Cup. In 1987 the team folded.'

Presentation night for Cauld Lad United FC. Wearside Combination League Division 1 KO Cup winners, 1970-71. Back row, left to right: Arthur Sawyer (manager), Arthur Carney, Jack the pub manager, Tom Foster (assistant manager), Dave Burnett, Denny Wilson, Billy Minnis, Alf Stubbs, Jim Owen, unknown. Front row: Brian Ainslie, Chris Hall, Keith Hambleton, unknown, unknown, Kenny Wilson, David Tucker and unknown.

Hylton Colliery Juniors, 1946-47. Winners of the Hetton Junior League, Horner
Cup, Strasbourg International Trophy, League Challenge Cup, North East
Durham Cup. Back row, left to right: Markham, Kirton, Howe, Fitzpatrick,
Milne, Waugh, Hibbert, Errington, Bell, J. De Roche (trainer). Front row:
R. Lee (treasurer), Kennet, Bewick, Bulmer, Cummings (captain), Tweddle,
Capeling, Clemmet and A. Bell (honorary secretary). In October 1947 Tom
Cummings (seated centre) signed for Burnley and he made 434 appearances
for them. Centre half Tom won a League Championship medal with the Clarets'
in 1960.

Rolls Royce FC, 1988. Managed by Tommy Dobbing (front row, extreme left)
and assistant manager John Wilson (front row, extreme right), this very
successful Washington Savacentre League side played at the Billy Hardy
Centre, Castletown. Their record between 1987-93 reads: Washington
Savacentre League Cup winners 1987-88, Washington Aged People's Trophy
1988-89 & 1989-90, Leukemia Cup winners 1991-92 & 1992-93, Clem Smith
Trophy winners 1990-91, Washington Savacentre League runners-up 1988-89 &
1990-91.

Wearmouth Colliery Welfare and the Miners' Strike

A cartoon from the *Football Echo*, 16th February 1952.

Wearmouth Colliery Welfare Football ground was opened on the site of the former Southwick AFC's ground by Mr T.E. Parrington, general manager of Wearmouth Coal Company, on Saturday 26th August 1933. The football ground was the first stage of a sports complex, which consisted of tennis courts, pavilion, bowling greens and caretaker's house at a total cost of £6,000. Colliery welfare work like the Wearmouth complex was being carried out throughout the country financed by the penny per ton levy on coal. Mr Parrington in his opening ceremony speech strongly criticized the poaching of players from colliery football clubs in County Durham by professional clubs: 'It is bad for the club. It is bad for the colliery as well, because my experience is that good footballers are always good workers. I am not blaming the club because I know it is helpless. I certainly do not blame the players who are anxious to rise to football of a higher status, but I do blame the all-powerful Football Association, which permits this wholesale poaching to go unchecked.' Wearmouth Colliery Welfare football ground was the venue of many local leagues' semi-finals and finals during its 40 years existence. The ground was sold in the mid 1970s and Coldstream Avenue was built on the site. In the late 1970s, or thereabouts, a football pitch was laid out on Wearmouth's Carley Hill cricket ground.

The bitter year long miners' strike that began in 1984 had an affect on Wearside Combination League side Wearmouth CW. Some of the striking miners, who were also players in the team, returned to work and other team members still on strike would not play with them. Outside players had to be drafted in to make up the team.

The groundsman too was brought into the dispute and he wasn't allowed to cut the grass. As the grass grew the cricket square was ruined and the football team played their home games on nearby Thompson Park. Wearmouth Colliery Welfare was also the venue for a soup kitchen where NUM members and associates were given meals.

Gordon Casey, Wearmouth CW Juniors, pictured on the Carley Hill ground during the miners' strike in 1984. Notice the uncut grass.

John Carty, manager of Wearmouth CW from 1984 to 1986, in his playing days for Southwick RAOB in 1972. The miners' strike posed team selection problems for John.

Hetton Youth League side Wearmouth Colliery Welfare Juniors in 1982, Durham County champions. Wearmouth played Lambton Street in the final and were trailing 0-2 at half time. In the second half Wearmouth rallied and forced a 2-2 draw to take the game into extra time when they ran out 4-2 winners. Back row, left to right: Gordon Miller, Peter Holehouse, unknown, unknown, Colin Russell, Chris Riley, David Edwards, David Holehouse, Alan Arkley, Wilf Cowie, Peter Holehouse Snr. Front row: David Carty, Paul Foot, unknown, John Dow (captain), Billy Todd, Charlie Crosby and David Cook.

A cartoon from the *Football Echo*, 23rd August 1952.

Boilermakers, Hetton CIU League, 1976-77. Back row, left to right: Tommy Clark, Joe Flett, Geordie Tansey, Thomas Callaghan, Kenny Redman, Geordie Crosby, Geordie Smith, Derek Jones. Front: Malcolm Clark, Billy Cruddas, David Callaghan, Keith Robertson, Keith Roberts and Brian White. Inset is John Shergold.

Tommy Clark recalls: 'John Shergold who established himself as one of the top managers in local leagues during the 1970s managed the Boilermakers. John assembled some of the very best players in the area and the Boilers was captained by classy defender Derek Jones, brother of Mick who was a professional footballer with Derby County, Notts County and Peterborough. Also included in the photograph are George Crosby who was the best centre half I had played with; the Callaghan twins, Thomas and David, were exceptional; Keith Robertson who was a FA Vase winner with Whickham FC in 1981 and Keith Roberts, a fast tricky goal scoring winger who would have moved into a higher class of football but for a serious knee injury which robbed football of a truly fine player.'

Hylton Castle Arms, early 1970s. Left to right: Bobby Cockburn (manager), Pat Tansey, Tommy Henderson, Bob Cockburn Jnr, Ron Henderson, Jimmy Green, Brian Close, Davie Elm, Jimmy Gibbons, Alan Hill, Billy Whittle and Kevin Woodhouse.

The Jolly Potter, South Hylton, 1984-85, Leukemia Cup winners, Ken Atkinson Memorial Trophy winners, Sunderland & District League runners-up. Back row, left to right: T. Butterfield (manager), S. Doran, S. Alcock, T. Laws, G. Flaxton, P. Martin, T. Liddle, D. Barker (secretary). Front row: A. Doran, J. Dow Snr, G. Mason (captain), J. Dow Jnr and K. Armstrong. Players missing from the photograph are: J. Appleby, T. Pallas and D. Watson. The Jolly Potter pub manager is holding the cups.

Sunderland Sunday League side Cheers, Premier League champions 2001-02. Players and officials named only. Back row, left to right: Liam Stoker, Geoff Moon, Neil Skaife, Dean Arkley, Steven Hope, Steven Dunlop, Stuart Burton, Ian Wardropper, Steven Stuart, Derek the physio. Front row: Lee Austin, Brian Rowe, Tommy Dobbing (assistant manager), Ian Loughlin, Gary Shields, Wayne Mullen, Shaun Godfrey, Joe Holborn, Mark Bute (manager), John Mordey (injured player). Inset is Steve Arnott (secretary).

Back cover photograph: Dagmar FC, Sunderland Sunday League Division One winners, mid 1990s. Back row, left to right: Davie Conlon (manager), Darren Drinkald, Mark Radcliffe, Paul Tench, Jonty Pemberton, Brian Conlon, Bobby Brewster, Davie Stobbart. Front: John Conlon, Ken Duggan, Sid Conlon, Chris Campbell, Gordon Casey, Dickie Conlon and Ian Conlon. Mascots: Billy Pemberton, Andrew King and Michael Conlon.

The People's History

To receive a catalogue of our latest titles send a large SAE to:

**The People's History Ltd
Suite 1, Byron House
Seaham Grange Business Park
Seaham, County Durham
SR7 0PY**

www.thepeopleshistory.com